AWAKENING *the*
NATURAL LOVE
of the HEART

AWAKENING *the* NATURAL LOVE *of the* HEART

Darshan Lotichius

CRYSTAL CLARITY PUBLISHERS Commerce, California

CRYSTAL CLARITY PUBLISHERS
crystalclarity.com | clarity@crystalclarity.com
1123 Goodrich Blvd. | Commerce, California
800.424.1055

ISBN   978-1-56589-347-4 (print)
ISBN   978-1-56589-509-6 (e-book)
Library of Congress Cataloging-in-Publication Data
  LCCN 2023049422 (print) | LCCN 2023049423 (e-book)

Cover design by Tejindra Scott Tully
Interior layout and design by Michele Madhavi Molloy

The *Joy Is Within You* symbol is registered by Ananda Church of
Self-Realization in Nevada County, California.

CONTENTS

Acknowledgements . . . . *vii*

Preface . . . . *ix*

Introduction: Why This Book?. . . . . *xi*

Part One

CHAPTER 1   A Sage for a Friend? 3

CHAPTER 2   His Own Scripture 7

CHAPTER 3   Introspection, a Key to Wisdom 11

CHAPTER 4   Removing the Log 14

Part Two
Removing the Eight Bondages

CHAPTER 5   Hatred 19

CHAPTER 6   Shame 26

CHAPTER 7   Fear 32

CHAPTER 8   Grief 39

CHAPTER 9   Condemnation 40

CHAPTER 10 Racial Prejudice 47

CHAPTER 11 Pride of Pedigree 53

CHAPTER 12 Smugness 60

Part Three
The Stages of the Heart

CHAPTER 13   Introduction to the Stages of the Heart. . . . 77

CHAPTER 14   The Dark Heart. 81

CHAPTER 15   The Propelled Heart 86

CHAPTER 16   The Steady Heart 91

CHAPTER 17   The Devoted Heart. 98

Part Four
Three Helpful Practices

CHAPTER 18   Introduction to Three Helpful Practices. . . 115

CHAPTER 19   Patience, to Transcend Time. 118

CHAPTER 20   *Swadhiyaya* — Deep Study 123

CHAPTER 21   Listening   130

Conclusion. 133

Further Explorations 140

ACKNOWLEDGEMENTS

My sincere gratitude to Joseph Siegel, whose editorial suggestions—professional and insightful—were available to me whenever greater clarity was needed.

I would also like to thank Mukti Hana Bozanin and Hansa Jennifer Black for proofreading the manuscript and for their useful comments.

And finally I'd like to thank my wife Madri for her encouragement, trust and love.

PREFACE

Y OU WILL MEET SOME uncommon actors in this book. Hopefully, you will come to regard them as your friends through reading their stories and insights.

The main character, *Swami Sri Yukteswar Giri*, will be extensively introduced in Chapter Two of the first part of the book. But a few introductory words about the other contributors might enhance clarity. Let me start with the narrator.

My spiritual name is *Darshan*, which means "he who tries to attain divine vision." My family name is Jan Lotichius. I was born and raised in Amsterdam, but I have spent most of my adult life in Italy.

Ananda Sangha is my spiritual community. It draws direct inspiration from the teachings of Self-realization as taught by my Guru, Paramhansa Yogananda, author of *Autobiography of a Yogi**, and a disciple of Swami Sri Yukteswar. This line of spiritual succession makes Sri Yukteswar my Paramguru — that is, the Guru of my Guru. Just as I enjoyed visiting my grandparents as a child, I often turn to him for counsel

---

* In this book all quotes will be from the reprint of the original 1946 edition of the *Autobiography of a Yogi*, by Crystal Clarity Publishers.

and consolation. His spiritual DNA flows uninterruptedly through my metaphysical veins.

Swami Kriyananda, born in Romania to American parents, and a direct disciple of Yogananda, is the founder of Ananda Sangha. I first met him in 1985, in Como, Italy. His friendship and guidance have since been the most important blessing in my life.*

And, last but not least, *Jesus* sometimes appears in these pages. In spite of his fame, he, too, should be introduced in this preface. For it is not so much the fame of his life and death, as the inspiration he has given — throughout the ages, to countless common people, artists, novelists, composers, and saints — that makes his presence ever new. I hope that my few humble stories about my own relationship with him will help you, too, to perceive him as a ray of that ever new light. ∞

---

* The reader might be interested to know more about the life of this remarkable man. Although his autobiography *The New Path* is not as widely known as Yogananda's, it can be rightly considered a complementary book: just as Yogananda wrote more about his master, Sri Yukteswar, than about himself, Kriyananda shares many inspiring stories about his guru, Yogananda in: *The New Path: My Life with Paramhansa Yogananda*, Crystal Clarity Publishers.

INTRODUCTION

Why This Book?

DURING CHALLENGING PERIODS, we often turn to friends or relatives for various forms of support: a listening ear, a shoulder to cry on, some words of encouragement. Who would deny that these gifts of love and concern can bring us relief from temporary distress?

Books, too, can console us. In my younger years, I spent many happy hours immersed in books by a writer who had left this world two decades before I myself entered it. Like my mother, he was born and bred in the Dutch Indies. During his early twenties he and his parents returned to Europe, where he led a life of restless soul searching, financial hardships, and literary experimentation. His writings were uncommon for his times, but when I read him, during my adolescence, it felt like he had written especially for me! The distractions of cellular phones and social media networks had not yet overwhelmed the world's stage, but even if they had, I hardly think they would have had the power to rob me of the precious time spent with this literary friend.

Truly good books are not only the well-written works of talented authors, they are also the fruit of personal processes of inner growth. They address the longer rhythms of life and individual philosophies that mature over time. Such deep and far-reaching conceptualizations rarely arise in normal conversation, even among dear friends.

So much of what really happens in our lives remains under the surface, like an iceberg. Can everyday discourse reveal anything at all about those intimate depths? That is where good books enter the picture.

True scripture is probably the most powerful form of literature. My first encounter with scripture happened at a very young age. By closing my eyes, I can still relive that experience. I am sitting in my father's armchair. My body is the body of a child. There's no one else at home and my only companions are perfect silence and a book that I have found in my father's bookcase. I am reading Jesus's sermon on the mount! My child-mind tries to decipher the ancient words printed on those old, thin pages. Conscious comprehension of this magnificent passage eludes me, and yet I am transported. I sense myself standing behind the vibrant orator, feeling the power that emanates from his body as he addresses his disciples.

Do not judge, so that you will not be judged. For in the way you judge, you will be judged; and by your standard of measure, it will be measured to you. Why do you look at the speck that is in your brother's eye, but do not notice the log that is in your own eye? Or how can you say to your brother, let me take the speck out of your eye, and look, the log is in your own eye? You hypocrite! First take the log out of your own eye, and then you will see clearly to take the speck out of your brother's eye! (Matt 7:1–5)

Although I can by no means say that I have always lived up to these words, I know that even then, as young as I was, I could sense their power. I was thrilled when I read them, without knowing why.

I was by no means a pious scholar. I loved playing and was occasionally mischievous, so this was an exceptional moment in my young life. But don't exceptions stand out more readily in our memory than rules and habits?

Indeed, scripture *is* exceptional: different from other good books that you might read while stretched out on the couch during a rainy Sunday, or in bed just five minutes before you fall asleep, or lazily lying on the beach. In true scripture every word vibrates with meaning. In order to perceive and receive it, we need to seclude somewhat, in a dimension beyond time and space where we can access the deeper layers of consciousness that scripture aims to address. Most people rarely do that. If they like reading, they often prefer texts that more easily mingle with the activities, interests, and challenges of their daily lives.

This book is meant to be a bridge between scriptural authority and those mundane everyday realities. Why am I using the unpopular word "authority"? I propose it because truth is either recognized or not. If it is recognized, it becomes a guideline, an influence, and thereby an authority. You can hardly argue with truth, nor would you want to do so, once you have begun to appreciate the life-giving nourishment and the joyful sense of freedom that it brings.

The first glimpses of truth will make you long for a kind of wisdom that does not just *reflect* on challenging periods in your life, but that takes into consideration *life itself* as the supreme challenge. While our parents have given us the gift of life, wisdom should somehow convey a method for us to transcend the mortality that comes with that gift.

And this can be done, the protagonist of this book tells us, by awakening the natural love of the heart. ∞

Part One

CHAPTER ONE

A Sage for a Friend?

WOULD YOU INVITE A person like Alexander the Great into your home? Would you welcome him into the family as a special friend in whom you could confide and who could watch the children, so that you and your partner can finally have an evening off? Could you talk to him about your struggles with addiction or depression, your marriage crisis, your longing for a partner?

Or would you tell him about favorable turns of events: the great choice that your teenage child has just made, the arrival of a long-awaited promotion, those moments of calm and poise that have come to you since you learned meditation?

Though Alexander was often victorious on the battlefield, he might not be the best choice for a leading role in the play of your life and relationships. His violent, disruptive energy, mighty as it may have been, could soon devastate your home and everything you hold dear. The stage could end up strewn with corpses.

While we certainly cannot ignore the overwhelming amount of energy that mighty Alexander possessed, we may be less than enthused about the *ways* he used it. The enormous amount of land that he conquered in fact constituted only a small percentage of the earth's total landmass, and the relentless hero's life ended before he could even begin to enjoy the fruit of his conquests. His physical body eventually died and became indistinguishable from the dust of the land he had conquered! His boundless ambitions were based on a tragic misconception: he was simply missing the point.

But he did change the course of history and could only have done so thanks to the enormous reserves of energy at his disposal. It takes energy to effect any significant changes in life.

The principal inspiration behind this book, of course, is not Alexander, but Swami Sri Yukteswar Giri, a master of yoga, who lived in India from 1855 to 1936. He became well known in the West mainly through the work of his foremost disciple Paramhansa Yogananda (1893–1952), who gives a thrillingly inspiring portrait of his Guru in his spiritual best seller *Autobiography of a Yogi*. There Yogananda writes:

> I often reflected that my majestic Master could eas-
> ily have been an emperor or world-shaking warrior
> had his mind been centered on fame or worldly

achievement. He had chosen instead to storm those inner citadels of wrath and egotism whose fall is the height of a man.

Can a sage, one who possesses such incredible energy—and hence magnetism—really be a friend? Can so much power and authority be reconciled with the equal standing that friendship implies?

This is an important question. In your Facebook community, or among your WhatsApp groups, you are unlikely to find the friend I am about to introduce. My hope, of course, is that you will find him through this book, and that you will be able to accept his authority, which was rightly earned. The "citadels of wrath and egotism" that he stormed had been his own, and yet his conquest has had universal implications. Once he obtained complete victory, no desire was left to control or dominate others. Thus he was able to say, with complete honesty, to his disciple Yogananda who had returned to him after a short period of desertion:

> Wrath springs only from thwarted desires. I do not expect anything from others, so their actions cannot be in opposition to wishes of mine. I would not use you for my own ends; I am happy only in your own true happiness.

That final freedom that Sri Yukteswar obtained through victory over ego, in a remote past, subsequently became the light that was free to shine through him and his teachings, thus illuminating many minds. My hope in writing this book is that it will also begin to shine on you, bringing back your enthusiasm for the pursuit of happiness, through wisdom.

CHAPTER TWO

His Own Scripture

S RI YUKTESWAR HIMSELF WROTE one book, named *The Holy Science*.* My own copy of it numbers barely a hundred pages. The booklet has been in my possession for over three decades and through all those years I often carried it with me during my countless travels, and, back home, kept it on the altar in my meditation room.

Many of its paragraphs I have read over and over again, partly to gain a deeper, intuitive understanding, but even more for the nourishment it gives to my soul. The author's spirit speaks to me through his book. I have always experienced Sri Yukteswar's complete self-mastery and friendship as kind, compassionate, and powerful.

Admittedly, it is not a very user-friendly scripture, mainly due to the prolific use of Sanskrit terms. Just as biologists

---

* *The Holy Science* by Jnavatar Swami Sri Yukteswar Giri, Self-Realization Fellowship.
  In this book I will frequently quote from my own copy, the eighth edition, 1990.

have adopted Latin to describe the world of species, Sri Yukteswar proposes the ancient Indian language, for spiritual science.

By that means, the author describes states of consciousness that, for the majority of his potential readers, remain out of reach. He speaks about *Lokas* (spheres of consciousness), about *Bhuvanas*, (stages of creation), about *Koshas*, or sheaths that envelop aspects of our consciousness. Though these concepts may be difficult to comprehend, you will unfailingly find that this Master, with the charm that comes with natural authority, magnetically draws his readers into an inner land of healing and assures us that we all have the capacity to access it, thanks to our highly developed nervous system.

In spite of its difficulty, however, the influence of *The Holy Science* on people and on spiritual and philosophical books that have been written since its first publication in 1894 has been enormous. An important seed was planted in that year, guidelines were set for spirituality in the new era and a bridge was built to cross the gap that threatens to separate science from religion and East from West.

Interestingly, the most quoted passage from the book is not the most difficult one. The author has already explained how feeling makes the world conscious, and how the center of this aspect of consciousness dwells in the human heart. And then he speaks about *the virtue of love*:

The heart's natural love is the principal requisite to attain a holy life. When this love, the heavenly gift of Nature, appears in the heart, it removes all causes of excitation from the system, and cools it down to a perfectly normal state; and invigorating the vital powers, expels all foreign matters—the germs of diseases—by natural ways (perspiration and so forth). It thereby makes man perfectly healthy in body and mind, and enables him to understand properly the guidance of Nature.

When this love becomes developed in man it makes him able to understand the real position of his own Self as well as the others surrounding him.

There are two ways to allow the deeper feelings of the heart to guide our lives once more. One is meditation, the other introspection. The two go hand in hand really, for it takes calmness to introspect effectively, and in order to meditate properly, we need to distinguish, resolutely, true from false in our mental and emotional chemistry, and focus, resolutely, on the former.

Although introspection is the main topic of this book, it would be good if, in the process of reading it, you could take some time to meditate. Just straighten your back at any time of the day and for five or ten minutes, watch

Mother Nature breathe through your nostrils. This practice will develop your muscles of concentration, calm your mind, and create an inner space for intuitive introspection.

CHAPTER THREE

Introspection, A Key to Wisdom

IN TRADITIONAL PSYCHOLOGY INTROSPECTION is practiced
principally to understand certain dynamics of the subconscious mind that influence our feelings and compel our
behavior patterns. There may be many: trauma, a genetic
tendency toward depression, bipolar disorder, and so on.
The idea behind it is, that once the diagnosis has been
made, we have gained some mental knowledge about ourselves. We know what it is that limits us, and we can learn
to live with it.

This type of recognition is accompanied by the possibility, at
last, to *speak* about what it is that hurts, scares, angers, or otherwise debilitates us. The suppurating wounds are looked at; the
pain is fully felt; the root cause is understood. A Dutch psy-
chiatrist during the sixties even injected consenting patients
with LSD, so they could relive the horrors they had suffered in
German concentration camps. The physician would guide
them through the experience and days later they would

listen together to the recording and introspect on it. Many of those patients have since testified of the healing effects this method had on their wounded psyche.

Methods like this address the problem where it is: in the arena of negative emotions. The rational mind, during the drug-induced, altered state of consciousness, retires back-stage. It is called back later, as the patient and his physician listen together to the recording of the session.

Diagnosing is in itself a mental process: it gives words, and sometimes labels, to dynamics that are essentially emotional and unseasoned. The raw materials of the subconscious mind are somewhat refined through the involvement of the rational mind.

At this point, however, a further question begs to be made: now that our mental imbalances have been safely labeled, now that certain difficult life experiences have become things of the past, is there anything else that we can do with the conscious mind? Or have we simply reached a plateau in our self-analysis, where we should be perfectly happy finally to be able to vocalize?

The spiritual psychology that is practiced in this book brings in an altogether different perspective. It highlights the importance of focus. It postulates that the mind assumes the characteristics of that which it focuses on. Diagnosis, in this perspective, becomes a form of inventory. The pursuit of wisdom through introspection only starts from there.

Maybe anatomy can be used to illustrate this point. On the battlefield of our daily lives, commander-in-chief Sri Yukteswar encourages us to keep the mind focused at the point between the eyebrows. "It will give you the power, the awareness, and the creativity to transcend," he says.

The alternative is to keep the mind belly bound by focusing on the depository of past pains and sorrows and allow them to compel our every move in battle. Once the blind spots have been detected, and the causes of our compulsive behavior understood, is it really necessary to linger in a limbo of mediocre rationalizations? Why not test teachings that train the mind to focus on higher states of consciousness as a means to win the battle?

A new horizon becomes visible, when we say, this is what the past has given me, now what shall I focus on?

CHAPTER FOUR

Removing the Log

> Love:
> O no! it is an ever-fixed mark
> That looks on tempests and is never shaken.
>
> — SHAKESPEARE

I N THE PREVIOUS CHAPTER it was suggested that we can gain the freedom to focus the conscious mind on subjects outside the problem-oriented subconscious sphere. This requires willpower, of course, but once the will is charged by enthusiasm for the subject that is being offered as an alternative, it will become our primary instrument for spiritual growth.

And how could there be no enthusiasm for a subject like the natural love of the heart? What a universe of bliss opens up, once we reawaken it through focus and proper introspection!

This is a general characteristic of spiritual discipline: it can never be imposed on our nervous system, yet something within us seems to recognize the need for it and assimilates it gradually and instinctively, until it naturally becomes ours.

Generally speaking, however, it is apt to compare the mind to the physical body: it needs exercise to grow in strength and to stay healthy. It will give us back what we feed it with. Science tells us that a prolonged and consistent focus on one or more specific subjects, creates new grooves in the brain that assimilate the subject in the subconscious mind where it becomes part of our habitual tendencies.

So what will be the focus of this book? For the next part it will be *the removal of bondage through introspection*. Sri Yukteswar lists eight impediments for true love to manifest in our lives: hatred, shame, fear, grief, condemnation, race prejudice, pride of family, and smugness.

Instead of making us ruminate about the past, introspection has now become like a navigation system. It serves to identify our position in relation to our goal, *a fixed mark*, and then to provide directions to take us there. If we, for any reason, fail to follow those directions, there will be no verdict of guilt and eternal damnation for us to fear. The system simply recalculates the position and provides new direction. And the goal—to free the heart of what oppresses it— remains unaltered.

In the next part of this book I will examine each one of these impediments. Together let us see to what degree they are present in our subconscious mind, and find strategies to remove them.

I have tried to be as informal and natural as possible. Sanskrit terms, otherwise so present in Sri Yukteswar's book, can be avoided here. They may become subject of another book about the author.

My hope is that you will enjoy the stories I share, that they will serve your own introspection, and that the journey itself will prove to be as joyful as the final discovery.

Part Two

REMOVING THE EIGHT BONDAGES

Learn to behave.

— SRI YUKTESWAR

CHAPTER FIVE

Hatred

> ... Love is not love
> which alters, when it alteration finds.
>
> —SHAKESPEARE, SONNET 116

THERE WAS A PERIOD in my life, sometime during my mid-twenties, when I was despondent because my girlfriend had left me. I simply couldn't comprehend how and why this had happened—and so unexpectedly!

Maybe the deep bond that I felt with her had eclipsed my awareness of residual effects of the traumas she had suffered during her dysfunctional childhood. Maybe she could already sense that I was on a spiritual path where she would be unable to follow me. Whatever had prompted her, the change came like a sudden, cruel blow; my pain was genuine and intense.

I found an opportunity to talk with a friend—a young American, a graduate in Psychology— who, like me, had come to Italy to be with her loved one.

"I don't understand," I cried. "All the love she first had for me has changed into hate!"

Her matter-of-fact answer surprised me. "It's the same," she said simply, without any further explanation.

Sometime later, I read *Samadhi*, a well-known poem that Paramhansa Yogananda actually wrote during a ride on the New York City subway. Clearly, environment was not an impediment for the rapturous inner journey of this great yogi! In the poem, we find a powerful expression of the ecstatic happiness that accompanies a limitless expansion of consciousness. "Memorize it," Yogananda used to tell his disciples, "for that is who you really are!"*

These are the verses that made me ponder:

> Love, hate, health, disease, life, death,
> Perished these false shadows on the screen of duality.

Are love and hate really the same then, as my friend the psychologist had said? Just shadows, both of them? And moreover *false* ones? My sadness left me enough space to ponder these questions. Memories related to experiences of love emerged from the past.

One of them regarded my older sister, who once confided: "Mom said to me that if Pop ever became unfaithful, she would start to hate him."

---

* The full poem was published in *Autobiography of a Yogi*, and in *Whispers from Eternity*, Paramhansa Yogananda, Crystal Clarity Publishers.

My then-teenage sister, who was introspectively inclined, enhanced her story with some comments of her own: "I think that's pretty superficial. *I* wouldn't hate him at all! *I* would try to *think* about myself and about him. *I* would try to understand!"

I, too, was trying to understand, and my despondency lent urgency to my spiritual efforts.

In *Autobiography of a Yogi*, Sri Yukteswar actually speaks about two manifestations of love—ordinary and divine:

> Ordinary love is selfish, darkly rooted in desires and satisfactions. Divine love is without condition, without boundary, without change. The flux of the human heart is gone forever at the transfixing touch of pure love.

For me, this grand promise and all its ramifications led to several realizations:

- If "ordinary love" is rooted in desires and satisfactions, then hatred can be the result of it. Such love brings expectations that no other human being can ever fully satisfy and it conflicts with the desire for freedom that is deeply rooted in every human heart. This leads to attachment, then frustration, a concomitant refusal to accept objective reality, a tenacious desire to change it, increasing restlessness, and finally hatred.

- If I could learn to direct my attachments upwards to
the spiritual eye, my capacity to accept and love others
(including my own immature self) would increase pro-
portionally and I would move closer to the *Samadhi* that
Yogananda described in verse. My heart would gradually become free, for in the Divine love that Sri Yukteswar
mentions, there is freedom.

Let's take a closer look at the other "false shadow" now, to
see if there exists something like "Divine hate."

Ordinary hate, like ordinary love, surely cannot fulfill any promise of complete satisfaction. Hitler's hatred
of Jews was human intolerance on a tragic scale. It was
true meanness — extraordinary in its scope of formidable psychic energy by which he involved a whole nation.
The big lie on which it was founded isolated him and his
people from humanity at large and from any satisfactory
unfolding of events. It could only lead to his eventual
destruction after a twelve-year cycle of national and international catastrophe.

In Hitler's intense hatred, there was no redeeming component of love for anything. Had he really believed in his own
theory of "blood and soil," he would have tried to save his
country from further bombings and ongoing war. Instead,
he used what had remained of his power to drag Germany
to destruction along with him.

But how about "divine hate"? Again, does that exist? Scripture seems to suggest it does . . .

The great epics from ancient India are goldmines of extraordinary stories. One of them, *Ramayana*, actually contains a story of divine hate!

It is the story of Ravana, a demon with very human tendencies, and his hatred of Rama, who symbolizes the Divine.

Ravana's passion for destruction had gained him a boon from Shiva, who, in India, represents God in His capacity of Destructor and Transformer. The boon was physical indestructibility!

This, however, did not even begin to give Ravana the happiness he craved—far from it! His human ego was afflicted with what Yogananda calls an "anguishing monotony." As centuries went by, generations came and went, and neither he nor anything else really changed. Filled with anguish, Ravana turned to Shiva once more.

Alas, the god of destruction could not help the poor devil, whom he himself had made indestructible. "Go to Vishnu," was his message. In India, Vishnu represents God in his aspect of Preserver.

Ravana then tried to escape from the net of anguishing monotony and tormenting restlessness by directing all his hatred toward Rama, king of the peaceful land of Ayodhya and an incarnation of Vishnu. He wanted to have what Rama had, so he began by stealing Sita, Rama's wife. Knowing that

Rama would soon be after him, Ravana organized a big army and set all his formidable powers against this gentle king.

Inwardly, Ravana probably knew all along that he could never win against God, the Only One. How can one destroy Cosmic Consciousness? But his hatred had become a veritable addiction: he kept trying, and his intense restlessness gave him the perseverance born of superstitious belief.

Eventually, this hatred led to his release. He was obsessed with Rama, and this fixation on God made him less and less human and more and more divine. In the heat of battle, Rama gradually killed the devil's human ego with all its torments, cutting it to pieces and eating it, bit-by-bit, until it became one with Himself. Now Ravana's indestructibility was no longer a physical, but a spiritual feature.

Success on the spiritual path does not depend on how good or bad you are, but upon the degree to which you can direct your energies (love and hate included) upward from the heart to the "liberating spiritual eye." In my own effort to do so, I often returned to Yogananda's ecstatic poem:

> Anger, greed, good, bad, salvation, lust,
> I swallowed, transmuted all
> Into a vast ocean of blood of my own, one Being!

I sought inspiration and guidance in teachings like these and was rarely tempted to enter the emotional arena of reactivity. I did not follow my ex-girlfriend's example and stayed away from hatred, love's opposite in the realm of duality. Gradually I came to accept love's sorrows in all its manifold manifestations, as a natural part of life. Now I am even grateful for the emotional setback that I suffered years ago. While that experience belongs to the past, the deep feelings involved imparted a lasting and cherished foretaste of the transformative power of love and compassion.

CHAPTER SIX

Shame

**Adam and his wife were both naked,
and they felt no shame.**

—GENESIS 2:25 (New International Version)

I'VE SOMETIMES WONDERED WHETHER it is shame that prevents us from being our best self. After all, living up to our highest potential entails the responsibility of dignity.

Years ago, I was part of a small group driving from Ananda Village, in the forests of Nevada County, to San Francisco. It was a long journey, so we stopped at a restaurant along the road for lunch. My friend, a young teenage girl who sat next to me, was the first to receive her order. It was a beautiful and delicious plate of spaghetti.

The other orders arrived, and we were ready to bless the food and start eating. Just then I heard a shriek of alarm next to me: "Oh my God, I can't believe I finished my plate in two seconds. You all haven't even started yet!"

I looked at my friend. She was blushing intensely and trying to cover her face with her hands. Her whole demeanor expressed intense embarrassment. In short, she was exhibiting all the terrible symptoms of shame.

Everyone tried to comfort her. I myself would have been the last person to judge someone for compulsive eating. At the same time, I could very easily understand the discomfort she was experiencing. What a hellish emotion shame can be!

In my early twenties, my own immature ego often suffered from stage fright, chronic insecurity, trembling hands, and episodes of sweating. For my fragile ego's presumed social failings and deficiencies at that time, shame was a regular companion.

In marked contrast to my social insecurities, and more deeply felt, my search for truth remained strong. I longed for something real in life but did not intentionally speak about this feeling with anyone. On occasion, however, my truth-seeking sentiments did filter into conversations among friends and acquaintances. If they reacted negatively to an earnest idea that fell outside their frame of reference for "normalcy," their opinions did not affect me.

Finally, help came. An old schoolmate of mine took me to visit a friend who lived on a houseboat in Amsterdam. A picture on the wall drew my attention. It was a black-and-white photograph of an oriental man with long hair. His eyes looked at me, piercingly and lovingly.

"Who is that?" I asked.

"That's Yogananda, of the Christ consciousness," my friend answered matter-of-factly.

I already knew somehow that yoga and meditation would become essential parts of my lifestyle. But now the Jesus whom I had loved as a little boy came back after a long journey out of my sight, to join hands with this magnetic figure whose picture looked at me so lovingly.

A few weeks later I visited that houseboat again, magnetically drawn by Yogananda's picture. The inhabitant, a practitioner of yoga and meditation, offered to guide me in a visualization.

"Lie down," he said. "Focus on the presence of Paramhansa Yogananda and listen for his voice." After a few more instructions, he lay down himself and began listening to my voice as I acted out a dialogue between me and the Master whom I had already recognized as my Guru.

Master's eyes spoke of his deep, unconditional love for me. Every time a thought arose of something that I felt bad about, I told Master and he counteracted that thought with an expression of his love. The conversation went on for quite a while. At the end of the dialogue, my friend and I could sense the light and energy that had filled the room.

After that experience, I felt better about myself. Some inner wounds had healed permanently. A process of self-acceptance had been triggered.

Over time, with each perusal of Yogananda's *Autobiography*

of a Yogi, impressions of Master grew inside of me like a lotus blossom. For instance, I came to appreciate ever more deeply the complete honesty with which he described his own moments of discomfort during his first public lecture on a ship sailing from India to the United States. His ordeal concerned his use of the English language; at that time, he felt that he had not yet mastered it to a point where he could give public lectures. There he stood, a Hindu with a turban, in front of his American fellow passengers:

> No eloquence rose to my lips. Speechlessly I stood before the assemblage.
>
> After an endurance contest lasting ten minutes, the audience realized my predicament and began to laugh.
>
> The situation was not funny for me at the moment. Indignantly I sent a silent prayer to Master [Sri Yukteswar].
>
> "You can! Speak!" His voice resounded instantly within my consciousness.

It seemed to me that what saved Yogananda during those difficult ten minutes was his faith in his Guru and his innate sense of dignity. I gradually came to realize that the love that was given to my very young self, during that special occasion with my friend on the houseboat, was really part of a much bigger picture in which self-acceptance and dignity played very important roles.

One's sense of dignity and self-acceptance needs to be maintained even under the most trying of circumstances. This requires practicing both when it's easy and when it may not be such an easy strategy, but as Yogananda would have said, it is certainly a victorious one.

For perhaps the root cause of shame lies within a deep layer of human nature. Didn't this all start with those poor, confused first ancestors of ours?

We all know the story: The snake convinces Eve to eat from the forbidden tree and she, in turn, tempts her partner to do the same. Then, as the story goes, God expelled them from Paradise.

But we can also look at it differently and ask: Who expelled whom?

The Bible says:

> And they heard the voice of the Lord God walking in the garden in the cool of the day; and Adam and his wife hid themselves from the presence of the Lord God amongst the trees of the garden . . . and Adam said to the Lord: "I heard thy voice in the garden and I was afraid, because I was naked; and I hid myself." (Genesis 3:8)

Until then the couple's paradise had been their closeness to God, who had created them in His own image and thus had conceived them as free to stay connected with His bliss, or to fall to lesser states of consciousness.

In spite of their transgression, if Adam and Eve had chosen to run back to God—naked, vulnerable, and unashamed—to tell Him what they had done, would He have rejected them? How could He? Didn't their nakedness make them once more a part of His own blissful Self?

Alas, they expelled *Him* from their consciousness, because from the position of their egos, they were ashamed.

Let us resist shame then by practicing calm self-acceptance. Let us offer ourselves unreservedly, unapologetically into God's caring embrace and Love. God himself tells us, through Krishna's mouth:

> But if in this [your spiritual efforts] thy faint heart fails, bring me thy failure!*

---

* The Bhagavad Gita is one of the most important scriptures of ancient India, in which Krishna, symbolizing God, counsels Arjuna, prince of devotees, about the yogic lifestyle. This line is quoted from Yogananda's translation of the scripture, published by Crystal Clarity Publishers.

CHAPTER SEVEN

Fear

Look fear in the face and it will cease to trouble you.

— SRI YUKTESWAR

A FRIEND OF MINE HAD always been a great admirer of the twelve-step programs, which are itineraries designed to guide people out of the labyrinth of substance and behavior addictions. He himself had never needed to participate in any of these programs, but after many years of meditation and soul searching, he made an interesting discovery. He, who had always considered himself to be free from compulsions, was yet addicted, to the physical body! Indeed, the mother of all addictions, he felt, is attachment to the physical body and to that part of individual consciousness that identifies with it, the so-called ego.

He then designed his own twelve-step program to free himself from this supreme addiction, and shared it with his friends—a very fascinating and helpful roadmap, indeed, consisting of meditation, introspection based on self-honesty, and attunement to a higher Power.

For the subject of this chapter, however, suffice it to say that the root cause of all fears *is* attachment to the body and to the material world. All fear is fear of loss: of life, health, reputation, money, control . . . dear reader, you are invited to continue this list for yourself!

It is probably the most debilitating of all emotions. The human ego at the height of its immaturity, holding on feverishly to anything it might lose, including its own, separate existence.

Ego, it should be mentioned, has nothing to do with original sin. It simply is a central human reality, that we need to work with on our way to bliss. It can be compared to a fruit. An unripe apple has a sour taste, but once it has reached maturity, it falls from the tree and is ready for consumption. This is a perfectly natural process.

"Nature never makes sudden leaps," science tells us. But that it does take the human ego in a gradual growth process, is shown by the fact that many fears that plague us during our childhood, are simply gone by the time we reach adulthood: fear of the dark, of separation from parents, of ghosts, etc. About such fears, Sri Yukteswar, in *Autobiography of a Yogi*, tells us the following story:

> My mother once tried to frighten me with an appalling story of a ghost in a dark chamber. I went there immediately, and expressed my disappointment at

having missed the ghost. Mother never told me another horror-tale. Moral: Look fear in the face and
it will cease to trouble you.

Admittedly, as we shall see now, other fears do not dissolve so easily in the process of growing up. New ones may
even emerge in our later life. Overcoming these becomes
part of our spiritual efforts. There is a lot of joy in it.

When I was in my late teens I made an unpleasant discovery: I had a fear of banks.

In itself this needn't have been a problem. But my friends
and I were traveling in foreign countries, and the special
checks that I was carrying needed my signature within a
bank in order to be cashed. Those blurred lines that my
shaking hands produced, could hardly be identified as human handwriting, let alone be proof of my identity!

I somehow managed to get to the end of those adven-
turous journeys, but try as I might, I could not, for the life
of me, understand where that misery-producing fear had
come from.

Well, if fear were a rational thing, one could reason one's
way out of it, right?

The thing is, such fear is as intensely paralyzing as it is
completely irrational, and even if we do find reasonable
explanations for its existence, that doesn't mean we have
overcome it.

As a young violinist I faced similar challenges. Serene experiences of musical expression could all of a sudden be threatened by a thunderstorm of stage fright that hampered the natural movements of my arms and hands.

How was I ever going to enjoy something like a musical career with such a treacherous and undesirable companion at my side?

When I was twenty-four I got a chance to speak about my problem with Swami Kriyananda, who had already become an inspiring friend and teacher for me through his books. Swami had heard me play some Bach and his own music, and he had thanked me for my ability to tune in so perfectly to his musical inspiration.

His response could hardly be called advice. Rather it was a simple, calm consideration.

He said two things:

- I think you will overcome stage fright in time, if you continue to play . . .

and . . .

- Practice pranayama.

"Pranayama" means the ability to sense and direct (yama) life force (prana). Sri Yukteswar and his line of yoga masters teach Kriya Yoga, a highly advanced form of pranayama. A prolonged practice of that science accelerates the natural process of inner growth and gradually weans the yogi from

addiction to the human body and from all the fears and
challenges that addiction can bring.

Not long after that conversation Swami himself initiated
me into Kriya Yoga. My journey to freedom from fear had
officially started.

Throughout the years, as my inner life began to develop,
I became less career oriented. Music simply became a form
of *sadhana**, an artistic opportunity to experience subtle aspects of sound. Communicating such a musical flow with
others became a purely joyful experience.

Over the years I have come to consider all fears as forms of
stage fright: God is the playwright, the director is the Guru
and we, in turn, are either good or bad actors.

Good actors are able to surrender themselves completely
to the flow of consciousness of their characters, without attachment to the role they are playing.

But such absorption, free of attachment, cannot happen,
if they themselves get lost in the emotional states they enact,
such as depression, elation, fear, and indifference.

A space of inner freedom is needed in order to act well. If
the actors were to become too identified with their characters' emotions, their free expression would be hampered and
they would risk a decline into bad acting.

A good actor is always happily aware of being part of
a creative process. He accepts and experiments with the

* Spiritual practices, such as meditation and prayer.

guru's directions and feels the loving, trusting eyes of the Playwright watching him.

So fear, indeed, turns us into bad actors.

The good news is that it can be overcome in time, as Swami says, if we but continue trying and if we practice pranayama.

Sri Yukteswar's teaching style has often been likened, by Vedic astrologers*, to the planet Saturn: slow, unemotional, self-contained, yet extremely efficient in making completely sure that we learn all the karmic lessons that our past foolishness has imposed upon us. Thus the maturity that Saturn brings is irreversible and becomes an enduring foundation for even the highest states of cosmic consciousness.

Sri Yukteswar's precepts are, in truth, only two:

- *Learn to behave!* . . . that is: be a good actor, attune yourself to the Divine Playwright and the role He has created for you . . .

and . . .

- *Let pranayama be your religion!*

Kriya Yoga, the highest pranayama, will help you create and safeguard the state of inner freedom you need in order to play your part in the world well. Life then becomes an exploration of God's infinite creativity and death a welcome break between your performances.

---

* The science of astrology, *Jyotish*, is part of India's most ancient scriptures, the Vedas.

Sri Yukteswar's final reassurance, if we follow his precepts, isn't even spoken in the material plane. As we struggle our way through our performances, memorizing our parts through the practice of Kriya Yoga, he keeps singing softly into our right, inner ear these lyrics of a chant he wrote:

*You won't have to fear anything, anymore!**

---

* The title of the chant is "Desire, My Great Enemy" and was published in *Cosmic Chants: Spiritualized Songs for Divine Communion*, Self-Realizations Fellowship.

CHAPTER EIGHT

Grief

You've been given a gift,
this profound connection to everything.
Just look for it, and I promise you it's there.

— ALLAN LOEB, screenwriter, in COLLATERAL BEAUTY*

THERE ARE THREE TYPES of grief—of the heart, of the mind, and of the spirit.

The heart feels what it feels. We can weave cocoons of denial around it; we can cover it with smoke clouds of mediocre reasoning; we can try to drown out its earnest whispers with restless noise. Still, the heart feels what it feels. Unless we calm down and learn to listen to what it is really saying, we will miss every chance to make substantial progress within ourselves.

I recently heard the following story about Lahiri Mahasaya†, the guru of Sri Yukteswar. This great nineteenth-century

---

* This beautiful movie about grief first came out in 2016.

† *Autobiography of a Yogi* contains an inspiring chapter about this great yogi: chapter 35, "The Christlike Life of Lahiri Mahasaya."

master of yoga lived an unobtrusive life with his wife and children in the ancient city of Varanasi, then called Benares. During the day he worked as an accountant in the Military Engineering Department of the Indian government. During the night he fulfilled his spiritual mission, initiating countless spiritual seekers in the ancient science and art of Kriya Yoga. Many of his disciples, including Sri Yukteswar, came to his home in the evening hours, to meditate at their guru's feet.

Lahiri's wife recognized her husband's divine state of consciousness and soon became his disciple too, but most of his other relatives were blind to his spiritual glory. Thus it happened that, when his daughter fell seriously ill, her husband's parents refused to allow their son's father-in-law to treat his own daughter by spiritual means, which the doctors considered to be unscientific. However, their own remedies proved ineffective in curing the young woman, who died shortly thereafter.

The night of her demise, Lahiri's disciples, respectful of the tragedy that had struck their guru's life, were reluctant to make any requests of him. They were understandably surprised to find him able to conduct the evening activities as usual, meditating with them, and occasionally offering words of instruction or encouragement.

At a certain point one of the disciples asked the master if he needed to be left alone with his grief. The master,

seeing in his eyes the amazement that stirred the defer-
ence, responded kindly:

> You don't understand. There is grief! Her death
> has struck this heart with grief, maybe even more
> strongly than it could any one of you who are present
> here. Yet your minds are like clay, sticky and heavy, in
> which life's unceasing ups and downs leave imprints
> that are difficult to eliminate. This mind, by contrast,
> is like a diamond, or like marble, in which no im-
> prints linger, not even of the greatest tragedies. This
> heart, though painfully struck, is still there for you
> all, to help you on your path of Kriya Yoga.

For people who are struck by tragedy, words like these
may well be difficult to comprehend, let alone to accept.
Their minds, furrowed with countless grooves of grief, do
not respond readily to a transcendent insight that calls for
such a radical change. Once the mind has embraced com-
plexity, it resists simplicity.

Yet might these words, which in no way deny the reality
of tragedy, indicate a shortcut out of the labyrinth of our
grief-stricken thoughts?

Let's look at other examples that may help us to understand this point. A personal memory of Swami Kriyananda
comes to mind.

It must have been sometime in the mid-1990s, when I was part of a small group spending informal time with him, a few days after his arrival from America.

The energy was high and joyful, as always in Swami's presence, and the conversation, free flowing. However, I knew about the challenges he had faced in America, where a lawsuit against him had been brought by self-styled enemies to destroy his reputation. So at a certain point I asked, "Swami, how did it go?"

"It was terrible," he answered, and in his eyes there was an expression of genuine grief.

Then the conversation continued as before, joyful and informal. But once or twice he repeated, "It was terrible."

In Yogananda's autobiography, too, we find instances of genuine grief. At the age of eleven, he lost his earthly mother. About that experience the author later writes:

> When we [father and I] reached our Calcutta home, it was only to confront the stunning mystery of death. I collapsed into an almost lifeless state.

If even great Masters like Lahiri Mahasaya and Yogananda and a close disciple like Swami had to experience such overwhelming grief in their hearts, why then does Sri Yukteswar list it as a *meanness*?

Authentic grief occurs when the heart realizes the depth

of love for the dear one lost, for the friends who betrayed us, for the partner who left us (or whom we left).

Beyond that grief there may even be a sense of gratitude for the full realization of that love, which all too often only reveals itself at the moment of loss.

In any case, it is a very deep feeling, not an emotion, usually best experienced in the solitude of one's own heart.

This type of grief is certainly not an obstacle; indeed, it puts our lives in a different perspective from which some wisdom might be gained. Moreover, the sense of gratitude for a love so deeply felt, along with the pain, can also become a step forward on our spiritual journey.

In order to understand Sri Yukteswar's point, we need to study how yogis are guided to relate to grief. There will always be, along with the grief, a natural desire to gain perspective, to focus on context. A student of Self-realization will give energy and focus to that desire.

Let's look again at Yogananda and his direct disciple.

The grief in Swami's heart was not so much about the lawsuit itself, as it was about the fact that his own fellow disciples had brought it against him. They had been with him at the Mount Washington headquarters in Los Angeles, when the Master was still alive. Those who knew Swami better have shared that there was grief around this issue, and that he allowed it to be rather than suppress it. But at the same time, he detached his mind from it, thus preventing complexes from forming. His mind and will were free to think and act with keen intelligence. Likewise, his heart was free to feel what it felt: grief at times, but primarily devotion and love for all those who came to him for guidance and inspiration, and full acceptance of what is truly happening.

That is what yogic self-control leads to in the longrun—a calm, free, and accepting heart.

During that informal gathering, Swami's mind was also free. He could shine his light with complete clarity on any subject of the conversation.

Yogananda relates how he, after losing his mother at such a young age, seeks final healing for his wounds:

> Years passed before any reconciliation entered my heart. Storming the very gates of heaven, my cries at last summoned the Divine Mother. Her words brought final healing to my suppurating wounds:
>
> "It is I who have watched over thee, life after life, in the tenderness of many mothers! See in My gaze the two black eyes, the lost beautiful eyes, thou seekest!"

For those who draw inspiration from Yogananda's life, the eventual success of his tireless spiritual efforts demonstrates that final healing comes from a higher power and that the spiritual path is a matter of life (with Spirit) or death (without Spirit). This process is what we may call "spiritual grief." We mourn, not for what we have lost, but for what we want to reclaim. Like a little child we cry for our Divine Mother, until She has no other choice but to satisfy our heart's desire. This basic attitude is expressed by Jesus, when he says: *Blessed are those who mourn, for they shall be comforted.**

Both Yogananda and his distinguished disciple used the strength of their minds so as not to be overwhelmed by grief for any longer than intended by nature.

Could it be, then, that Sri Yukteswar refers to *mental* grief as a meanness, not *of*, but *to* the heart?

If the mind is not kept under control, a false grief can develop—a self-pitying habit of focusing on things that happened a long time ago and that bear no productive relation to the present. Such a habit will increasingly sap away all powers of initiative.

How can we prevent grief from becoming a habit of the mind that goes on forever? Here are some possible strategies:

- Try to use impersonal language. Instead of saying "I am mourning," one can say impersonally "There is grief in this heart."

- After an initial period of mourning, see if it helps to speak about it less. Always be selective in choosing the people with whom you share your feelings.

* Matt 5:4

- Allow the grief to be, when it arises, but use your will to focus the mind on other, uplifting realities of "collateral beauty." In other words, use your willpower—not to repress feelings, but to detach the mind from them.

- Life is short and our days are numbered. "The spiritual path is a matter of life or death." Therefore, let's try to take heart from Yogananda's example, by using the techniques he and Sri Yukteswar have given us, as a battle horse and armor "to storm the very gates of heaven."

And finally:

- Trust the heart's power to heal from within. It is endowed, Sri Yukteswar says, with "natural love, the heavenly gift of nature."

If this is true, then nature and spirit, humanity and divinity, live together in our hearts. The divine aspect naturally brings nourishment and healing, if we but develop enough willpower to prevent the mind and the ego from interfering.

CHAPTER NINE

Condemnation

> First take the log out of your own eye,
> and then you will see clearly to take the speck out of
> your brother's eye!
>
> — JESUS (Matt 7:5, NEW AMERICAN STANDARD BIBLE)

I HAVE THE GOOD FORTUNE to live near Assisi, where the grounds are hallowed by the presence of Saint Francis. You don't need to be religious to feel, inwardly, an atmosphere of joy—a treasure that is difficult to find in this world. Countless pilgrims throughout the centuries have been inspired by this place. Swami Kriyananda beautifully describes their experience:

> I understood anew the value of pilgrimage: going to places not only to see, but to inwardly commune. Feeling the divine sweetness of Saint Francis, I wondered: How is it possible for anyone to be so utterly sweet? Then the answer came: by never

judging anyone; by being from one's heart a brother
or a sister to all; by complete humility—but above
all, by never judging.

Condemnation works like a boomerang. Whatever we,
compelled by emotion, criticize in others, we will have to experience personally ourselves—either in this life or in some
future incarnation—to the degree of intensity of the emotion
that we invested in our condemning thoughts. I can share an
interesting experience that may highlight this teaching.

A major karmic challenge in this life arose during my early school years. One day a boy emerged from a large group
of children playing in the schoolyard. He walked over to me
and said, "We are friends." His announcement was accompanied by a rather fierce handshake.

The so-called friendship that ensued for Edmund and
me from that abrupt introduction was tinged with diffi-
culties. At the time, I was interested in music and reading
beautiful books. In secret, I tried to know more about Jesus.
This innate interest had little or nothing to do with the
non-religious family into which I was born. At an early age
I knew the happiness that comes with deep enthusiasm and
complete absorption.

Conversely, Edmund's emotional framework was too
fractured and tormented to go deeply into anything. His
eruptions of envy and anger kept his consciousness limited

to the surface of his being. His favorite strategy was an attack from behind. All of a sudden, I would find myself lying on the street stones with Edmund on top of me trying to hit me with his clenched fists.

And yet, for whatever reason, I felt compelled to be his friend. It was not unlike the way in which people under the yoke of tyranny feel obliged to love their nation's leader. These feelings of compulsory love can never be genuine, of course, for love requires freedom.

I experienced Edmund's tyranny of unbridled emotions as a continuous source of discomfort. For several years, I was unable to extricate myself. At the same time, mysteriously, the adults in my life, such as parents and teachers, consistently turned a blind eye to my ongoing predicament.

Edmund followed me to high school, but by then I had found the strength to distance myself from his aggressive energy. During some unusually open conversations, I was even able to sympathize with him as he told me about his parents' divorce and his father's desertion.

There was one dramatic moment that I recall with particular clarity. We must have been eighteen or nineteen at the time. He ran over to me (not from behind this time), looked into my eyes with great intensity and exclaimed, "You have always judged me!!!"

Those words stuck with me, not emotionally, but spiritually, as if they had awakened some ancient soul memory.

Years later, a highly intuitive astrologer, looking at my natal chart, said, "It looks like you had to endure some extreme bullying in your early childhood. You do have a well-developed sense of justice, but in some previous incarnation you may have been a very harsh judge of some kind, applying severe punishment systems and showing little mercy."

These two items of unfavorable karmic information became important signposts in my life.

As I am writing this story, I am visiting my mother in Amsterdam, the place of my birth. As is my custom during such visits, I am meeting up with some friends whom I have known ever since I was young. As far as I know, they are not yogis—at least we never speak about the themes that are the subject of this book. Nevertheless, in my heart they each hold a special place, especially one of them.

As Richard spoke to me last night about his house, his book collection, his trouble with his neighbors, I observed the tendencies of my thoughts. "He is worldly," they said, "so this is not spiritually inspiring company for me. He's materialistically attached to his things."

I also noticed a certain impatience in listening to him and the inner efforts of my conscientious self to find a way out of this downward spiraling energy.

"See God in everyone," the teachings say. Well, I wasn't able to do that. *My* damning verdict had already been reached: attachment, materialism, worldliness!

In an effort to change perspective, with inward vigor I focused my mind at the point between the eyebrows—the seat, yogis say, of higher states of consciousness.

All of a sudden, a new perspective emerged. I could feel Richard's deep affection for me, and along with it, my deep affection for him. "He is trying to say something deeper," a voice whispered.

"He needs your unconditional acceptance. Do not circumscribe his spirituality with your own definitions of him. Instead, listen with that deep feeling you have always had for him. Don't feel superior to him, just because you meditate and live in a spiritual community."

As my heart accepted this line of thought, my energy and my mind came back under the guidance of my higher Self. I was able once again to be there, fully present with him like in the old days but more conscientiously. A renewed sweetness infused the companionable evening that we spent together.

By judging other people, we nail them to our own rigid definitions of them, thereby discrediting their potential for spiritual unfoldment. It's not that we should become blind to other people's defects—we simply no longer react to them with careless or repressive emotion. We discriminate but we do not judge. Instead, we accept.

Emotionally biased judgments are subconsciously conditioned by things of the past: a difficult family, traumatic episodes suffered at school, and many other negative experiences constitute the ball and chain we carry with us in our adult lives. Observing ourselves dispassionately in our tendency to judge others, will be like the mirror we look into every morning. It will diminish the weight of the ball and the substance of the chain, until it finally breaks. Then other people will no longer need to take the blame or make amends for all that we have perceived as hurts and setbacks in the past.

Only full and unconditional acceptance of *all* the actors, past and future, appearing on the stage of our lives makes it possible for us to give the best to our family, colleagues, and friends. Overcoming the meanness of condemnation, then, will reveal itself as a true path towards Self-realization.

CHAPTER TEN

Racial Prejudice

The beauty of anti-racism is that you don't have to
pretend to be free of racism to be anti-racist.
Anti-racism is the commitment to fight racism
wherever you find it, including in yourself.
And it's the only way forward.

—IJEOMA OLUO*

IN HIS INTRODUCTION TO *The Holy Science*, Sri Yukteswar gives a majestic description of the four astrological eras our planet goes through as the sun, dancing with a twin star millions of light years away, makes its vast circular journey through our galaxy, gradually moving away from its grand center, and then approaching it again, from another direction.

These eras are four in number, he says, and they represent as many stages in human evolution.

We have just exited the lowest stage, named Kali Yuga, and have entered the second one, known as Dwapara Yuga.

* American writer, author of *So You Want to Talk about Race*, Seal Press 2018.

In Kali Yuga, we perceive reality principally through our senses. Our consciousness is imprisoned within thick walls of matter. Happiness is sought in sense pleasures, which are, inevitably, followed by their opposite state: pain.

A more important hallmark of that era—we cannot see beyond appearances.

Racism is a legacy of Kali Yuga. It judges people, not by the content of their character—to quote Dr. Martin Luther King, Jr.—but by the color of their skin. As we move deeper into Dwapara Yuga, the age of energy and content, we will find ways to transform this demeaning legacy, but a lot of work remains to be done.

A detrimental result of the emotional inability to see beyond appearances, is the idea that one race or ethnic group is more evolved—and therefore better—than other races, and that the "superior" race therefore has the right to control, or even suppress the "inferior" race, just as man also wields control over species of the animal kingdom. According to this fallacious reasoning, the difference between races remains insurmountable, because certain physical characteristics, mainly skin color, do not change as a person grows towards maturity.

This prejudice is actually much subtler than one would think. I have heard of a quiz especially designed to detect traces of racism in a person's mind (or brain grooves). A friend of mine, after many years of meditation, tried it out and discovered she had to make quite a few corrections in her thinking and take the test many times before, finally, her results were completely negative!

The main reason why truth seekers, of all countries, need to face and overcome this meanness in their own heart, lies in the fact that the final purpose of any spiritual search is to attain Christ-Consciousness—the ability to perceive Divinity equally in everything and everyone. Once God starts smiling lovingly at us through the eyes of all our fellow human beings, can there still be any prejudice left? And as long as the heart's deeper feelings are suppressed by prejudice of any kind, can Christ smile at us from every corner of our world?

Let us then focus on some of the deeper causes of this meanness and on possible ways to uproot them. As we do so, it is important to remember that it is never a good idea to fight against an opposing force. In antagonism there usually is an emotional animosity that weakens, rather than strengthens, our fighting force. In any psychological battle, the best weapon is calmness. In that sense, therefore, I am not truly an anti-racist in the terms expressed by Ljeoma Oluo. I simply consider racism to be a dangerous infection of man's spirit, and I try to use introspection to bolster my "spiritual immune system" against this disease.

Let us introspect together, then. Here are some possible root causes:

Mass karma: White supremacy is not just the recent movement in American society that many associate it with. It is the philosophy at the base of many centuries of European colonialism, of which the suppression of Native Americans and the rise of slavery on the American continent were only a part. In fact, the recorded history of the world up to our times includes many stories of peoples conquering and then dominating other peoples. The current migrations of individuals from former colonies to countries of former colonizers is a karmic consequence of centuries of white supremacy. As those countries occupied in the past suffered under foreign domination, people born in the West are now reminded, subconsciously, of that suffering and therefore feel uncomfortable sharing their country with immigrants coming from those parts of the world.

Possible remedy: Remember that, in our pursuit of happiness through wisdom, we must learn to transcend the influences of the world, which include any negative form of mass karma. Therefore, instead of reacting emotionally to the karmic changes that are happening in your country, focus inwardly on core values like individual freedom and justice for all. The more you embody those values with your own growing wisdom, even without talking about them, the less you will be affected by negative influences around you. You will become a positive, causative power, rather than a leaf helplessly tossed around by the winds of mass karma. As Swami Sri Yukteswar says in *Autobiography of a Yogi*:

> The deeper the self-realization of a man, the more he influences the whole universe by his subtle vibrations, and the less he himself is affected by the phenomenal flux.

Fear of change: As we shall see further on in this book, change is life's way to help us evolve and expand our consciousness. Though it is often experienced as an invasion of our comfort zones, when we accept it wholeheartedly, we can also experience the inner freedom and joy it brings. The blend of cultures and ethnicities that is now occurring in the world may strike many people as a threat to their own egoic comfort zones. Yet it is the breakdown of those predilections that opens the way to full spiritual unfoldment.

Possible remedy: Forsake victim consciousness! There is no power at all in laying the blame on changing circumstances and on other people—so called foreigners—for our own perceived misfortunes. In marked contrast, there is a lot of power in seeking security and safety in our own soul. Affirm with Yogananda: *I will seek safety first, last and all the time in the constant inner thought of God-peace.**

---

* *How to Have Courage, Calmness and Confidence* by Paramhansa Yogananda, Crystal Clarity Publishers.

Mistaking emotions for ideas: Many so-called political ideas are really negative emotions, such as fear or anger, in disguise. Pure ideas possess causative power, but emotions create nothing but chaos and block progress of every kind.

Possible remedy: Practice introspection and be very honest with yourself. Observe yourself when you speak about politics, religion, or even child education. Are you really expressing ideas, the fruits of experience and long pondering, or are you merely stirring the air with vapid chatter?

It is a sign of dishonesty to continue to talk—or think—politics, when the real job to be done is to recognize the restless emotions in the heart and then calm them through some form of yoga practice. Opinions are usually worthless. They refer back to the emotional state of the speaker who expresses them, and not to ultimate reality, which they break into disconnected little pieces. Worthwhile ideas in any field of knowledge—politics, psychology, philosophy, sociology, etc.—spring from the deeper feelings of the heart and are the natural fruit of a long, comprehensive inner search for truth and understanding, based on resolute introspection.

The simplest way, however, to let go of any lingering remnants of racial prejudice in your heart, is to observe and accept this: We have entered Dwapara Yuga, an age of free-flowing energy and inspiration, too subtle to be stopped by barriers such as walls, religious bigotry, attachment to old ways, emotional nationalism and, yes, racial prejudice.

And we should not remain blind to the signs of the times.

The Holy Science was written by Sri Yukteswar for the purpose of bringing East and West together in an exchange of knowledge and cooperation. He trained Paramhansa Yogananda for the same purpose. Upon his disciple's departure for the West he said to him, and through him to all of us:

> Forget you were born a Hindu, and don't be an American. Take the best of them both. Be your true self, a child of God. Seek and incorporate into your being the best qualities of all your brothers, scattered over the earth in various races.*

CHAPTER ELEVEN

Pride of Pedigree

I do hate the aristocratic principle of blood
before everything, and do think that as reasoners
the only pedigrees we ought to respect
are those spiritual ones of the wise and virtuous,
without regard to corporal paternity.

— From TESS OF THE D'URBERVILLES, by THOMAS HARDY

THERE IS NOTHING WRONG with being happy to belong
to a certain family, community, social class, or nation.
Every individual needs a social base to work from and to
relate to. Our spiritual progress will be tested first by our
ability to relate appropriately with those who are near us:
family, friends, and colleagues. If any of these individuals are
excluded, even to the slightest degree, from the natural love
we seek to awaken in our hearts, there can be no substantial
emotional and spiritual growth.

But the feelings connected with belonging frequently become stirred or agitated. Then that sense of belonging may

become a mental issue, with thought-forms that, to some degree, set our group apart from other human beings. The group then becomes a clan, which comes to define itself by the adversarial emotions that it cultivates towards other clans.

In this process, loyalty becomes impassioned instead of calm, clarity goes out of the window, and a meanness develops that will suppress the heart's natural love. Sri Yukteswar simply calls this pride of pedigree. Its presence in our consciousness may vary from subtle to pronounced.

Years ago, after a happy, healing stay of three weeks at Ananda Village in Northern California, I decided to leave without saying goodbye. It was poor form, certainly, and I made it worse by writing to one of my friends whose feelings had been hurt: "My father always said, parting must be short and unemotional!"

I've never forgotten that friend's response. She wrote: "That shows me again how people copy their parents' behavior patterns, instead of acting on their own feelings."

Facing the emotion of parting with courage and an open heart would certainly have been a more expansive way for me to relate to her feelings and those of others, but I hadn't been willing to make that effort. And then that same emotional carelessness moved me to justify my behavior by proudly quoting my father. But in this situation, he was just one of the six or seven billion people populating the earth, with no connection to the feelings of those involved.

Yogananda said: *Loyalty is the first law of God*. With regard to family and country, this guideline means that we should first be loyal to the core values that hold those social groups together in a meaningful way, as long as these values spring from true inspiration and connection to a higher power. Thus a loving mother reminds us of the mother aspect of God; a wise father, of His wisdom; a country, of the inspired wisdom of its constitution. If we never lose sight of these core values in relating to our communities, then our loyalty can indeed become a basis of the powerful righteousness Yogananda describes. But if our loyalty is tied instead to individuals or groups only, it can easily become emotional and, in the process, lose its positive, causative power.

As I drove a friend of mine to the airport the day after her full day of counseling in our Ananda Assisi community, she said to me, "It was a bit much; but I must say, the person I have in front of me is always the most important one in the world."

This might actually be a good strategy for overcoming pride of pedigree: to see potential divinity in whoever happens to be with you or near you at any time, giving them some form of special, heartfelt, spiritual attention—a prayer, a smile, a listening ear, anything appropriate for the occasion.

Try to imagine an excellent, highly professional counselor whose teenage son is acting up badly, possibly owing to substance abuse or some other peer-related challenge. Imagine further that this counselor has had a very hard weekend with his family. Now it's Monday morning, he's back at work, and a new client shows up for a first, introductory session. That client turns out to have a teenage son with problems related to substance abuse.

Wouldn't the counselor's integrity be measured by the degree to which he can put his personal worries on a shelf and be fully there for the unique situation and needs of the client? Can he keep full control of any emotional association that might arise in his heart, between his client's son and his own?

Does such a professional responsibility make you less loyal to your own people? That could arise if you reserve your integrity for your work alone, while allowing your personal life to be influenced by all sorts of subconscious motivations. But if you refuse to be a dilettante in *any* area of your life, then your vigilant awareness will create a joyful, solution-oriented magnetism that will not fail to have a positive impact on *all* the people you interact with. It will also increase your power to be fully there for them and *with* them when they need you.

If you learn to control your emotional reactions in relation to your dear ones, you are leaving them free to explore their own consciousness and deeper feelings. What greater sign of love and loyalty can there be than that? But as long as there is a disproportionate attachment to form, name, and pedigree, your ego will claim your loyalty, and the road to soul freedom and happy relationships will be blocked.

For centuries, royal families in Europe, anxious to maintain purity of bloodlines in their clans, arranged marriages among their own relatives. This practice not only gave rise to all sorts of mental and physical diseases, it also made them completely unable to relate to the reality of the peoples they were supposed to govern. In fact, when one's family name becomes the only merit that supports one's position of power, what motivation can there be to use it for the good of the people?

George Washington, the general who defeated the army sent by King George III of England, was also the first president of the United States of America. He retired after serving two terms as president, thus showing that he was more dedicated to the principles on which this young country was founded than attached to his own position. Upon hearing this news of Washington's willing abdication of power, the King, bound to his position by pride of pedigree, exclaimed with the frustration that often accompanies genuine admiration: *If he does that, he will be the greatest man in the world.*

In our new age of Dwapara Yuga, there is the so-called American dream: the possibility for one with very humble origins to make it all the way up to the highest office in the country. Isn't such an individual much more likely than the mentally unbalanced king to possess the wisdom to preside over a government "of the people, by the people, for the people"?

Pride of pedigree falls under the government of ego. As you may have inferred from the above accounts, I think that Sri Yukteswar, who always encourages us to be relentlessly honest in our introspection, assigns a wider and subtler significance to this meanness: a tendency to place merit where it doesn't belong and the emotional turmoil that is caused by this form of self-deception.

Furthermore, by "pride of pedigree" he may even have meant: a tendency to place the *blame* where it doesn't belong. If arrogance and shyness are two sides of the same egoic coin, so are pride and an inferiority complex.

Some people have issues with their families that persist for a lifetime. They may blame their parents for many bad things that they have done—and which might actually be true. They may experience their family DNA as a burden and even wish they had been born into another family. They may see all sorts of undesirable characteristics in their own children. This might be called: *bound* by pedigree.

The root cause for this meanness is non-acceptance of reality. The solution lies in a constant spiritual effort to accept people, all people, as they are. This solution is by no means a passive attitude. It requires much more energy than most people realize, for the acceptance should be of the heart, not of the mind.

The mind should be kept free to see people as they are: an alcoholic father, a daughter not living up to one's expectations, even people coping with traumatic family situations. But the heart should learn to accept all this as a manifestation of the law of karma, which allows no room for victim consciousness of any kind. The good news is that, once the mind begins to acknowledge how deeply the heart rejoices in this practice, the journey to complete soul emancipation is fully under way.

It may also help to meditate on the following words from the Festival of Light, a text written by Swami Kriyananda to be read as a part of Sunday services:

> And whereas suffering and sorrow, in the past, were the coin of man's redemption, for us now the payment has been exchanged for calm acceptance and joy.

Sometimes, when I feel that this calmness and this joy are almost inaccessible, I think of these words from Yogananda's autobiography about his Guru.

> My relationship with Sri Yukteswar, somewhat inarticulate, nevertheless possessed a hidden

eloquence. Often I found his silent signature on my thoughts, rendering speech inutile. Quietly sitting beside him, I felt his bounty pouring peacefully over my being.

Can such bounty ever come to us as long as our heart is troubled by racial prejudice or bound to the past by pride of pedigree?

CHAPTER TWELVE

Smugness

"The workers who were hired about five in the afternoon came and each received a denarius. So when those came who were hired first, they expected to receive more. But each one of them also received a denarius. When they received it, they began to grumble against the landowner. 'These who were hired last worked only one hour,' they said, 'and you have made them equal to us who have borne the burden of the work and the heat of the day.'

"But he answered one of them, 'I am not being unfair to you, friend. Didn't you agree to work for a denarius? Take your pay and go. I want to give the one who was hired last the same as I gave you. Don't I have the right to do what I want with my own money? Or are you envious because I am generous?'

"So the last will be first, and the first will be last."

— JESUS (Matt 20:9-16, NEW INTERNATIONAL VERSION)

WHILE MY SPIRITUAL COMMUNITY can hardly be called "institutional," its group endeavors do entail organizational efforts. However, it is not rules or regulations that hold our family together, but rather the individual attunement of most of our members to the ideals of plain living and high thinking. Other guidelines are a commitment to the spiritual growth of the individual, adherence to truth, and daily practice of meditation. Most of our members accept these guidelines willingly, simply because they feel inspired by them!

Our ministers offer guidance and friendship, but they hardly give directives. Leadership positions are viewed as a responsibility and an opportunity to serve.

Given this lack of institutional governance, starting an Ananda meditation group can be an arduous enterprise that requires deep attunement with the above mentioned ideals and guidelines. Founders have to develop the ability to listen to true inner guidance, which is possible only if the ego is kept at bay. Errors will inevitably be made, but with them also arises the opportunity to learn from them. All this makes an established meditation routine indispensable.

Many years ago I myself was involved in the founding of an Ananda center in Rome. Although I scarcely had any prior experience with starting a facility like that, my enthusiasm was intense and sincere—but it was not always kept under control.

Yogananda encourages us to interiorize our spiritual enthusiasm so that we might apply it judiciously. Properly cultivated and applied, it can lead to powerfully beneficial results. Like dynamite, it can dig tunnels through many layers of ego, towards the center of our own being.

Clearly, I still had much to learn about spiritual enthusiasm.

My fellow disciples in Rome were likewise sincere, but aligning our personalities was an ongoing process. Harmonious cooperation, indispensable for the building of a spiritual work, offers daily evidence of the degree to which the individual devotee has transcended his ego. He may feel deep calmness in meditation, only to find that, in interactions with other people, his calmness flies out the window and smug ego steps forward to take charge.

On one occasion, in a meeting with my team members, I remember claiming my seniority: I had been with Ananda Europe since its beginnings; I had met Swami Kriyananda many years earlier; etc. Smugness was expressed more in the tone of my voice than through my words. As I spoke, I could feel a downturn in the compliance of my fellow disciples. "What's next?" one of them asked, somewhat ironically, after I had finished my presumptuous discourse.

Subsequently, I came to realize the meanness of this attitude. It affirmed the ego and made me incapable of relating lovingly to other peoples' realities, thus distancing me from an objective that, deep in my heart, I longed for. It also degraded my inner attunement with Swami Kriyananda himself, which was even more painful. Swami had always defined harmony as one of Ananda's main goals, smugness posed a formidable barrier to achieving that end.

Fortunately, our sincere efforts and Swami's prayers for Divine grace prevailed. Meditations, satsangs, and kirtans were organized, teachers were trained, and by now, thanks to the steadfastness of its founders and core members, Ananda Rome has become an important center in Italy for the dissemination of Yogananda's teachings.

There is also a more universal need to overcome smugness. Dwapara Yuga, the age of energy that is mentioned in a previous chapter, signals the end of institutionalism and the rise of the individual. In the coming centuries, people's confidence in institutional claims and protection will diminish significantly until, eventually, the only security left will be their own intuitive perception of the degree of integrity within the individuals whose company they keep.

Ananda Sangha can be regarded as a landmark and a standard in this evolutionary process. Positions are important only to the degree to which those who hold them give them meaning with their own spiritual growth, as channels of light. Anything less than that is simply not appealing.

However, in the early dawn of Dwapara (Sri Yukteswar states that this era only started in the year 1900), memories of Kali Yuga—with its rigid, hierarchic, and dogmatic thinking—still cling to us. Smugness, therefore, becomes a meanness to overcome at all costs. Here are a few guidelines that might help you in the process:

- Avoid speaking about your spiritual practices and experiences. Instead, keep them intimate, between you and God.

- Try to make yourself useful and, regardless of the position you hold, define your dignity by the degree in which you let your ego dissolve in the flow of service.

- Expand your sense of respectability. Let your self-respect depend less on social decorum and expectations, and more on your own innate sense of proportion and propriety.

- Pray for your superiors as well as your subordinates and learn to listen with equal, full attention to both.

- If your position is important, try to find small, inconspicuous ways to serve as well, without mentioning them.

- Make meditation an act of listening and then apply that principle in your cooperation with others.

- Often meditate on Jesus' fierce criticism of the Pharisees and on his words: "the first shall be last, and the last shall be first."

In the final analysis, keeping clear of smugness is a way to protect and experience the deeper feelings of the heart. In this way, intimacy, so often sought mistakenly in a tumultuous relationship between egos, leads instead to communion with nature and to inner wealth and happiness.

Part Three

THE STAGES OF THE HEART

Nature doesn't make sudden leaps.

— GOTTFRIED LEIBNIZ

CHAPTER THIRTEEN

Introduction to the Stages of the Heart

Stop and consider! Life is but a day.

— JOHN KEATS

M Y SON'S FIRST YEAR at junior high school was anything but easy. In addition to making the necessary adjustments to this new cycle of schooling, he also attended the conservatory in another city, which entailed many hours of train travel each week. That same year, he participated in at least four classical guitar competitions. His mother and I had developed a decent level of co-parenting, and I had the honor and the joy of having him with me during the last two weeks of that intense adventure. He had brought some important homework assignments, including writing a report of his overall evaluation of the entire school year.

Unnoticed by him, I watched as he sat at the dining room table—thinking, writing, and then thinking again—with a serious expression on his face and his pen in his left hand.

After a few hours he asked me if he could read his report to me. In the process of writing, he had felt trapped in countless details, and the list of all his activities and engagements was long indeed. The last paragraph brought it all back to the present. I was deeply touched as I heard him read:

"It was a very busy year, with many engagements, too many I sometimes thought. But now, as I look back, and as I look at myself, I realize that I have grown."

Even as I write this, many years later, I get tears in my eyes—my little boy, only eleven years old, experiencing the joy of self-discovery!

This realization, of course, came at the end of the school year. It is very difficult to assess a growth process while we're in the middle of it. By the same token, we don't dig up a seed every day after planting it to see if it is sprouting, but we rejoice when we see the first hints of green rising up from the soil.

The cycles of human development are, as we know: infancy, childhood, adolescence, adulthood. With some metaphysical banter, these could be interpreted as follows: In infancy we need to regain control of the physical body, and in childhood, our emotions; during adolescence we become fake adults, and during adulthood we *are* fake adults, heedlessly following the ways of a world that seems utterly devoid of any meaning or lasting purpose. In fact, this period from early man- or womanhood through old age is marked by the quiet desperation mentioned by Henry David Thoreau. And finally death puts an end to the show.

The bleakness fades from this sorry rendering, however, if we change our perspective and understand that human growth does *not* stop with the end of our adolescence. By attuning ourselves to spiritual inspiration, we can continue to grow, until our ego, like a mature fruit, falls from the tree. Then we might truly earn our credentials to be thoughtful adults, and more than that. And what a joy it is, that the possibilities for Self-realization can be discovered at *any* time in our lives!

As we have said before, it can be difficult to measure growth while we are still in the process. It isn't effective for an athlete to stop in the middle of a match to see if he has won. He will make his assessments at the end of the game.

To help us assess our own state of consciousness, Sri Yukteswar gives us a roadmap that identifies five different phases of spiritual growth. He calls them the stages of the heart and describes four of them: dark, propelled, steady, and devoted. Then he mentions the clean heart, but that can no longer be considered a stage. At that point, we have reached our journey's end in timeless, infinite Presence. The ego, our little self, falls like a ripe fruit from the tree, and at last our higher Self can arise.

Let us then "stop and consider," as Keats enjoins us in his famous love poem, the characteristics and the possibilities of each of these stages. In the process, we will gain a sense of direction and reach decisions that can carry us closer to our goal. This has, throughout the ages, been the function of spiritual introspection.

CHAPTER FOURTEEN

The Dark Heart

And the light shineth in darkness;
and the darkness comprehended it not.

—JOHN 1:5 (KING JAMES VERSION)

THE PATH OF SPIRITUAL introspection is not necessarily an easy one to travel by—sometimes winding and uphill, other times straight and smooth; sometimes bright and tranquil, other times dark and beleaguered by ambushes. It is surely never paved, and although roses can be seen and smelled along the path at times, their thorns, too, are keenly felt.

The darkness we speak of here, is not the one that disappears as the sun rises. Doesn't it rise in the sky every day above most places on earth? And yet how many of us, children of the earth, gratefully contemplate this ever new wonder and absorb it in our lives? Instead, we might nostalgically hold on to darkness, wrapping it around us like a fur coat on a sunny day.

At this stage, pain and pleasure are experienced primarily on the physical plane, through the senses. Perceptions of reality remain confined to the material universe. Sri Yukteswar calls this state of consciousness and everyone in which it prevails, *Shudra*. A *Shudra* sees the brick stones of which a beautiful building is made, but may fail to appreciate the vision underlying its beauty and the energy invested in its construction. At best such a person may idealize the building as a good hiding place or as protection against a perpetually hostile world.

We all carry something of this *Shudra*, or at least the memory of him, within us. We are aware enough to recognize the pain he brings. Although we may have mostly transcended its dark realities, it can still be experienced as our pain.

Indeed, living in the "bliss" of ignorance brings about long-term effects that can extend far beyond the span of one incarnation and might manifest in mood swings. The mind that revels in intense temporary sense pleasures, will inevitably be dragged down by the opposite experiences of emptiness, disgust, and torturous restlessness.

Paramhansa Yogananda, Sri Yukteswar's direct disciple, said the following about moods:

> They are caused by past overindulgence in sense pleasures. They are the consequence of over-satiety and disgust. Don't give in to them . . . if you indulge

in moods, they will reawaken your past desire for their opposite pleasures. Thus, they will pull you down into delusion again.*

So, if you suffer from moods in this life, you can now recognize them as outgrowths of the residual darkness that our hearts have all experienced or, to some degree, are still experiencing.

One particularly pernicious mood is commonly called depression. This has become somewhat a superficial label, like ADHD or bipolar. The inevitable result is that we look at the label and forget about the individual, who alone, uniquely, possesses the keys to the type of healing (s)he needs. In fact, I myself was a bit prejudiced against the term, and against all labels, until an interesting experience taught me some compassion.

I was staying with an elderly couple in a little cottage near the North Sea, in the Netherlands. The sea was grey and wild; dark clouds were passing swiftly in the sky, propelled by a storm that seriously compromised every mental effort to focus. The moon, the sun, and the stars seemed to be gone forever.

My friends were downstairs, drinking a bottle of wine and watching the news, which was depressing as usual. Although

* From *Conversations with Yogananda* (Passage 235), by Swami Kriyananda, Crystal Clarity Publishers.

still young, I was already a yogi. Not wanting to interfere in their choices, I went upstairs and started to pray.

I was used to receiving some type of positive response to my prayers, especially in the form of sweet intimacy with a divine presence, but this time something else happened. All of a sudden I found myself energetically and emotionally clogged. My willpower received a blow and lay wounded in a corner. A dark feeling of gloom and despair entered my system.

Fortunately, the silent observer within me, trained by years of dispassionately watching the breath, had survived the blow. He observed the situation and then calmly said: "This is depression, and it's difficult."

Since then, I have no longer repudiated people's use of the term "depression" for themselves or for others.

If you are now struggling in an abyss of gloom, cheer up! There is some good news for you.

To paraphrase Sri Yukteswar:

> All the Shudra needs to do is to secure the company of some more highly evolved human being. That association alone will give him the strength to take a first step up the road towards enlightenment.

If you are reading this book, you have found, in Sri Yukteswar, the best possible company you can imagine.

All you need to do is think him near, look at his picture, call him in prayer, and study his teachings, which can be aptly summarized in his following words of solace and encouragement:

> Forget the past! The vanished lives of all men are dark with many shames. Human conduct is ever un-reliable until anchored in the Divine. Everything in future will improve if you are making a spiritual effort now.*

---

* Yogananda, *Autobiography of a Yogi*.

CHAPTER FIFTEEN

The Propelled Heart

The secret of genius is to carry
the Spirit of the child into old age,
which means never losing your enthusiasm.

—ALDOUS HUXLEY

T HE OTHER DAY I was counseling a friend. Our conversation started on a positive note. After a period of neglect, she wanted to resume her career as a holistic healer again. Many creative ideas about how to promote her services came to her, and she shared them willingly with me. Inspired by her enthusiasm, I offered some suggestions myself. After twenty minutes or so she seemed ready to start. She had a plan!

But then the conversation shifted to the difficult divorce she was going through and the energy changed considerably. All the elements of pain and turmoil arose in her delivery: anger, jealousy, indifference, grief. It was sheer suffering.

A mutual friend had suggested that she should try to create a safe, physical distance from the man whose role in her life was now shifting from husband to ex-husband, and to see him as seldom as possible. Let space and time be your instruments of healing, she had said. But this was difficult advice to follow, for the two separating spouses were also co-parenting a child—their child.

Suddenly an idea came to me. I heard myself say, "You could go to Paris or New York and have a glorious time, but he and the whole situation would still be on your mind and weigh on your heart. The only distance you can take from it all is by focusing on something else. You have just shared all these wonderful insights about your career. Why not follow your enthusiasm and take your next career steps? That will surely make you gain perspective, and hence renew your strength to cope with the situation! And in the meantime, try to bear with it."

She agreed with me and after some more talk about the healing power of meditation we shared our farewells. Interestingly her first appointment for that day was related to her healing work. She had an online session with a client.

The light shineth in the darkness, says John at the beginning of his gospel. "Shineth" is archaic English for "shines." This verb tense, although it is called the Present Simple, does not refer so much to what is happening right now, as to what happens normally. "The light shines," in other words, means that that light is constantly there, and our first step out of the darkness occurs when we catch a glimpse of it. If, after that, we are inspired to progress further, we must try to maintain and expand our focus on that light.

In my early forties, quite unexpectedly, I felt propelled to have my Dutch university degree recognized here in Italy. I immediately acted upon this unforeseen objective and fearlessly challenged the labyrinth of this country's bureaucracy. Finally, I was told that, in order to get what I wanted, I had to pay a year's university fee, take three additional exams, and rewrite my thesis.

The exam subjects were Latin, human geography, and poetry. My heart was filled with an inexplicable enthusiasm.

To be sure, enthusiasm is by its very nature inexplicable. It is a deity (*theos*) that *en*ters the human heart and gives us wings to fly.

While fulfilling my duties as a husband and a father of two children, I made use of the nighttime to withdraw from my family so as to dive deeply into the literary heritage of the ages and to explore the human landscape. Enthusiasm gave me energy, clarity, and strength of memory. I rewrote my thesis, passed all the exams with flying colors, and . . . that was the end of it! I never got to make any practical use of my newly gained certificate, which was thus reduced to a mere piece of paper.

Still, what a wonderful power enthusiasm is! Lifting us up, at least temporarily, from the mud of body-bound needs and desires, enthusiasm leads to a freedom that allows us to focus on something different from and greater than ourselves. A little light relieves the dark heart, at last.

In the beginning, the visiting deity may be of a lesser kind, giving us creative ideas that reinforce, rather than transcend, the constrictive ego. That, too, is a step forward for the suffering heart.

Generally, society looks upon worldly ambition much more favorably than upon mere sense pleasures, which often carry an element of shame. Ambition, in contrast, gives rise to the myths of success and of money and fame.

But more importantly, an evolutionary power underlies ambition. In order to fulfill an ambition, we need to put out some form of creative energy. This creates magnetism, and the magnetism makes us grow.

Eventually we become strong enough to respond creatively to the pain of disillusion that, sooner or later, follows the fulfillment of each ambition. During an interview, the highly successful movie director Roman Polanski said with candid hindsight: *My career is OK, but it hasn't given me bliss.*

The greatest blessing is to become enthusiastic, not about academics or other worldly endeavors, but about spiritual teachings that guide us to seek happiness within, rather than in the world. The pursuit of happiness, then, becomes the pursuit of wisdom. In the process, Sri Yukteswar can be our guide if we think him near. It still requires a lot of energy. The great Gyanavatar (a title bestowed on him by Yogananda, meaning "incarnation of wisdom") describes the process of the seeker, regardless of gender:

> His/her heart then becomes propelled to learn the real nature of the universe and, struggling to clear his/her doubts, (s)he seeks for evidence to determine what is truth.*

He then writes that, once this undertaking has become our *natural duty*, we are on our way to finding permanent fulfillment.

In my own soul-felt process, poetry has become a romance with inner sounds, images, and intuitions; geography, a study of inner landscapes. They are like rivers that, through my absorption or baptism, will lead me back to a recognition of the highest of all gods, our own reflection of Divinity. When lesser passions are carried away by streams of disillusionment, that reflection remains within me.

Can we realize all this in the turmoil of modern life? Sure, why not? As we study and practice teachings that uplift us, our unfolding spirituality will allow us to fulfill our duties creatively and lovingly. The inner quest brings us to a point where we can sit down every day, straighten the back, breathe deeply and calmly, meditate and gratefully affirm: *I am free now, I have life more abundantly, like a mighty river, within.*

* Yukteswar, *The Holy Science.*

CHAPTER SIXTEEN

The Steady Heart

In the realm of ideas everything depends on enthusiasm...
in the real world all rests on perseverance.

— JOHANN WOLFGANG VON GOETHE

I WAS ALREADY AT UNIVERSITY, when I learned that one of my high school mates had died of an overdose of heroin. He had been one of many in my school who used drugs in their teens, but most of them put them aside at some point, and went on to become successful lawyers, doctors, scholars.

Still, how dreadfully vulnerable those teenage years are! I have often wondered, sadly, why it is that some adolescents survive, at least socially, whereas others end up in the gutter, or dead. Years later, a passage from *Education for Life,** Swami Kriyananda's book about a new approach to schooling, brought some clarity:

---

* *Education for Life: Preparing Children to Meet Today's Challenges*, by J. Donald Walters, Crystal Clarity Publishers.

A friend of mine one day, struggling in the quick-sand of a negative mood, was attempting to define everything in life in terms of the general hopeless-ness of it all. He challenged me to say something that would make him see things differently. And of course, though I tried, my best efforts proved un-availing. For when a person wants to be unhappy, no one in the world can make him happy.

But then an inspiration came to me. "I'm not re-ally worried about you," I said. "We all have a certain specific spiritual gravity, and return to it repeatedly and naturally after any period of temporary depres-sion or euphoria. All that's required is that we relax into ourselves again. Your own specific gravity," I said, "is high. I'm sure you'll return to it naturally in a day or two without any help from me."

And so it proved.

It was a useful inspiration. In the world of physics, objects rise or sink, as we all know, according to their own specific gravity relative to the density of the me-dium surrounding them. A child's balloon, if filled with helium, will rise as soon as the child releases it, and will continue rising until its own specific grav-ity is of the same density as that of the atmosphere around it. An object placed in water will sink, if its

specific gravity is greater than that of water, but will
float if it is less.

People too, I've noticed, sink or rise in their consciousness according to another kind of "specific
gravity." Some natures are naturally heavy; others,
naturally light.

People with a naturally positive outlook may rise
above even extraordinary set-backs — tests under the
impact of which other people, more pessimistically
inclined, might sink without a trace.

This book actually became like a scripture for me, during
the eight years that I myself taught at an Education for Life
school. In my interactions with children I always tried to
assess their specific gravity and approach them according-
ly. Many a disharmonious situation, such as can arise in a
group of children, were thus prevented. Our children felt
that they were seen, understood, and accepted according to
their present state of consciousness.

In the material world, the specific gravity of the chem-
ical elements cannot be changed, at least not according to
our current level of understanding. This, of course, begs the
question: Can the specific gravity of consciousness change
in a human being? Does it become heavier or lighter as the
years go by?

This may very well depend on our life direction. If the main focus is on the world and on social conformity of any kind, specific gravity may actually increase over the years, just as many people gain weight when they get older. We may become disillusioned, for example, when our deeper feelings are ignored. An increasing feeling of heaviness sets in, which reaches its culmination with old age.

In his early teens, my father was a fervent opponent of European colonialism in what was then called "the Dutch Indies"—an archipelago which, like a garland of emeralds, winds about the equator. Not surprisingly, his views also opposed those of my grandfather, who was of the opinion that "we (the Netherlands) simply cannot afford to lose our colonies."

But only a few years later, when the Dutch—recently liberated from five years of Nazi occupation— launched a military campaign to invade and reclaim "their" lost colonies, my father's political views had drastically changed. He had grown critical of Soekarno and Hatta, the leaders of the Indonesian resistance, calling them "criminals," and supported the crimes of the Dutch army in a country that had never truly been theirs. What had happened?

Assuredly, love was the determining factor in his change of heart. My father had fallen in love—passionately and romantically—with a girl who had moved to the Netherlands shortly after the end of World War II. Upon seeing her and experiencing the shock of love at first sight, he made some inquiries and found out that she had been born in the Dutch Indies. There she, like all the other colonialists, had been imprisoned in a Japanese concentration camp.

My father now dreamed of visiting the exotic land where his sweetheart had spent her childhood, a dream that might well become impossible if that land lost its Dutch identity and became Indonesia. In my father's heart, political justice and personal, romantic attachments had become unduly intertwined.

Enthusiasm, as we said in the previous chapter, is a deity (*theos*) entering the human heart. It brings euphoria, but over a longer period of time, it can also bring disappointment and depression. This simply depends on the source of our enthusiasm.

Many of us may have experienced some manifestation of romantic teenage love. The tears shed for first love's sorrows are sometimes remembered nostalgically as a counterpoint to adult life's challenges: the crying babies and dirty diapers, electricity bills, estranged adolescents, mortgages, marital quarrels, bitter divorce, and old age. What remains, then, of the enthusiasm of our younger years? Is it really meant to wither and die?

For enthusiasm to become a steady undercurrent of joy, we must fall in love—not with a schoolmate, but with a true spiritual teaching. It must beckon to us and lead the way out of the material land of duality and into an inner dimension of Spirit, lasting peace, and transcendence. This transformation will be the *real* end of the foreign colonization of our true homeland within.

When you are a spiritual seeker, you are also a scientist. You can only learn from your own experience, so you must experiment. When you are blessed to chance upon a true teaching—and to recognize it as such—you will still want to make inner notes about what works and what doesn't work. The discernment required for this scientific job can only be cultivated by regular meditation.

I myself, after finding my own Guru many years ago, have had to find my way out of quite a few karmic entanglements, human love being only one of them. Yet one memory stands out like a lighthouse in a stormy sea.

I was in my car, on my way to see my kids, who lived with their mother. It was a challenging period of financial stress, professional insecurities, and the pain of living far away from my children. To distract my attention from my gloomy thoughts, I put on an audio cassette of Mozart's *Laudate Dominum*.

Suddenly, in the middle of a forest road, I had to stop my car, for I could feel a crying spell coming over me. How surprised I was to feel tears of gratitude flowing over my face! *Such a beautiful life, Lord*, I kept repeating. *Thank you, thank you!*

Many years of strenuous spiritual effort, of integrating my Guru's teachings into all aspects of life, had yielded its fruit. My heart had become steady, and the most important part of my consciousness would remain untouched by "the slings and arrows of outrageous fortune."

Do not these words by Sri Yukteswar, remote as they may seem from the current reality most of us live in, sound like a promise—difficult to understand, and yet giving us hope for a better, more luminous future?

> Following affectionately the holy precepts, he (man) learns to focus his mind directing his organs of sense to . . . the door of the internal sphere. There he perceives the luminous body of John the Baptist, or Radha, and hears the holy Sound (Amen, Aum), like a stream or a river; and being absorbed or baptized in it, begins to move back to his Divinity . . . *

* Yukteswar, *The Holy Science*.

CHAPTER SEVENTEEN

The Devoted Heart

How many loved your moments of glad grace,
And loved your beauty with love false or true,
But one man loved the pilgrim soul in you,
And loved the sorrows of your changing face.

—WILLIAM BUTLER YEATS

AMERICANS OFTEN FINISH THEIR phone calls with relatives by saying "Love you!"

These two words, or three ("I love you"), or even five ("I love you so much!"), also pop up frequently in other contexts, such as a mother greeting her child upon return from a first scout camp, away from home. Or after the mother's own return from a long business trip, with feelings of guilt for having been away from her child for so long.

Words or short phrases may become inflated and empty, when they are used all too frequently. Another significant example of this is "Jesus Christ"—a combination of name and title that identifies a spiritual Master. However, it often springs like an insult from the mouths of people who have little or no relationship with that Master. Similarly, the phrase "for Christ's sake" often expresses the speaker's exasperation rather than an appeal to the Light that Christ can bring. I hear careless uses of these phrases so often that I've had to discipline my mind to preserve the deeper, more intimate meaning that Jesus holds for me.

Still, it can be a good thing to be able to affirm love with a short, habitual phrase, capable of diminishing or avoiding disharmony, "I don't agree with you, but I love you; I've been away for some time, and I missed you, because I love you so much; I have to go, but I really don't want to leave you, because I love you so much; I'm saying these things because I love you!"

When you add melody to those words, some of their deeper meaning returns. I remember Yoko Ono, in an interview, speaking about her famous husband, shortly before he was killed: "It's still very important for John to be able to sing 'I love you.'" Many years after his death we can still feel that significance, when we listen to him singing those or similar words.

Sri Yukteswar, however, sheds an altogether different light on this topic. In Yogananda's *Autobiography of a Yogi*, we read about his first meeting with his guru. At the time, he went by his childhood name, Mukunda. The scene is highly symbolic. A busy marketplace in the Bengali section of the city of Benares represents the world, where people of all backgrounds are buying and selling wares. But Mukunda's eyes notice a niche unseen by all the others: in a narrow lane he spots "a Christ-like man in the ochre robe of a Swami, standing motionless." Drawn magnetically to him, he leaves the busy world and walks back to the narrow lane:

> My quick glance revealed the quiet figure, steadily gazing in my direction. A few eager steps and I was at his feet.
>
> "Gurudeva!" The divine face was none other than he of my thousand visions. These halcyon eyes, in leonine head with pointed beard and flowing locks, had oft peered through gloom of my nocturnal reveries, holding a promise I had not fully understood.
>
> "O my own, you have come to me!" My guru uttered the words again and again in Bengali, his voice tremulous with joy. "How many years I have waited for you!"
>
> We entered a oneness of silence; words seemed the rankest superfluities. Eloquence flowed in soundless chant from heart of master to disciple. With an antenna of irrefragable insight I sensed that my guru knew God, and would lead me to Him. The obscuration of this life disappeared in a fragile dawn of prenatal memories. Dramatic time! Past, present,

and future are its cycling scenes. This was not the first sun to find me at these holy feet!

My hand in his, my guru led me to his temporary residence in the Rana Mahal section of the city. His athletic figure moved with firm tread. Tall, erect, about fifty-five at this time, he was active and vigorous as a young man. His dark eyes were large, beautiful with plumbless wisdom. Slightly curly hair softened a face of striking power. Strength mingled subtly with gentleness.

As we made our way to the stone balcony of a house overlooking the Ganges, he said affectionately:

"I will give you my hermitages and all I possess."

"Sir, I come for wisdom and God-contact. Those are your treasure-troves I am after!"

The swift Indian twilight had dropped its half-curtain before my master spoke again. His eyes held unfathomable tenderness.

"I give you my unconditional love."

Precious words! A quarter-century elapsed before I had another auricular proof of his love. His lips were strange to ardor; silence became his oceanic heart.

"Will you give me the same unconditional love?" He gazed at me with childlike trust.

"I will love you eternally, Gurudeva!"

"Ordinary love is selfish, darkly rooted in desires and satisfactions. Divine love is without condition, without boundary, without change. The flux of the human heart is gone forever at the transfixing touch of pure love." He added humbly, "If ever you find me falling from a state of God-realization, please promise to put my head on your lap and help to bring me back to the Cosmic Beloved we both worship."

Yogananda then proceeds to describe the years of training he underwent in his Guru's ashram, confronting and gradually accepting the relentless discipline he received there.

When I had abandoned underlying resentment, I found a marked decrease in my chastisement. In a very subtle way, Master melted into comparative clemency. In time I demolished every wall of rationalization and subconscious reservation behind which the human personality generally shields itself. The reward was an effortless harmony with my guru. I discovered him then to be trusting, considerate, and silently loving. Undemonstrative, however, he bestowed no word of affection.

Silently loving, but no words of affection — no "Love you," no "I love you," no "I love you so much!" A quarter-century later, Yogananda, after fifteen years of sharing his Guru's teachings in America, returns to India. The chapter dedicated to that visit, called "Last Days with my Guru," contains one of the most touching episodes in the whole book.

"Guruji, I am glad to find you alone this morning." I had just arrived at the Serampore hermitage, carrying a fragrant burden of fruit and roses. Sri Yukteswar glanced at me meekly.

"What is your question?" Master looked about the room as though he were seeking escape.

"Guruji, I came to you as a high-school youth; now I am a grown man, even with a gray hair or two. Though you have showered me with silent affection from the first hour to this, do you realize that once only, on the day of meeting, have you ever said, 'I love you'?" I looked at him pleadingly.

Master lowered his gaze. "Yogananda, must I bring out into the cold realms of speech the warm sentiments best guarded by the wordless heart?"

"Guruji, I know you love me, but my mortal ears ache to hear you say so."

"Be it as you wish. During my married life I often yearned for a son, to train in the yogic path. But

when you came into my life, I was content; in you I
have found my son." Two clear teardrops stood in
Sri Yukteswar's eyes. "Yogananda, I love you always."
    "Your answer is my passport to heaven." I felt a
weight lift from my heart, dissolved forever at his
words. Often had I wondered at his silence. Realizing
that he was unemotional and self-contained, yet
sometimes I feared I had been unsuccessful in fully
satisfying him. His was a strange nature, never utterly to be known; a nature deep and still, unfathomable to the outer world, whose values he had long
transcended.

Strange to tell, in my younger years I was somewhat skep-
tical about this scene, thinking: Why would a great Master
like Yogananda need such confirmation from his Guru?
And why would the Guru be so emotional about it? In other
words: *How can they be so human?*
    Over the years I have come to realize that there can be no
divinity without humanity, and that it is their humanity that
completes the greatness of these two men — highly evolved,
and marked by the intuitive, wordless bond they share, untouched by distance in space or by the passage of time.
    Let's ask ourselves honestly: Can the love between two
egos ever fully satisfy the heart? I remember — years ago, in

the company of Swami Kriyananda and a group of devotees from Rome—attending a conference given by an acquaintance. This man's sentimental message was, "Let us all love each other and be kind to each other." To make his point, he had taken a devotional chant by Kriyananda and changed the words so that they would fit his philosophy. The original words were:

> My heart is Thine, always Thine, Lord
> Singing to You
> Loving You
> I live in a heaven of joy.

Our friend had changed the object of his love, from God to his girlfriend. He sang Kriyananda's melody with the following words:

> I love you so much
> I sing it to you
> I love you
> And that makes me happy!

We devotees from Ananda Rome were somewhat mellowed by this conference. For a week or two, we tried to bring more harmony into our honest attempts to cooperate with each other, including a final note of "I love you" on our phone calls, such as this presenter had encouraged and many Americans do. But then, during a lunch with a few of us, Kriyananda gave his view on this type of communication. He had not appreciated the man's rendition of his devotional song, and added, "I hardly express love explicitly, with words. Rather through my actions. And my first attentions always go to God, the source of all love. By contacting Him first, His love can flow through me to other people. That love alone can transform them. My love alone, by comparison, would barely scratch the surface."

Love for God, religiously speaking, is devotion. Devotion is feeling, steadied by focus. It is love plus commitment.

It is important to understand, that this does not in any way diminish the importance of human love. Nature herself has deeply planted the need for human love in our hearts, especially in the form of the mother instinct. On a more physiological level, this instinct serves the survival of the species. No living, conscious being can survive without some measure of maternal love. It is not simply being the fittest that enables survival—as Darwin has stated—but rather the bond between mother and infant.

Sri Yukteswar does not separate nature from God, but neither does he focus on its mere physiological aspects. Instead, he identifies the spiritual essence that underlies Nature and calls it by a beautiful Sanskrit word, *Prakriti*. This is how he describes it in *The Holy Science*:

The Almighty Force, or in other words the Eternal Joy, which produces the world; and the Omniscient Feeling, which makes the world conscious, demonstrate the Nature of God the Father.

The feeling that makes the world conscious—these powerful words bring back a memory. Long ago my youngest son, age five at that time, asked me, out of the blue, "Dad, do you exist?"

"Yes," I responded, without thinking.

The answer, I now think, was just as interesting as the question, coming out of the mouth of a little child.

What made it interesting was its immediacy.

Of course I exist! A thousand fleeting joys, a thousand heartaches, a thousand hard lessons to be learned, and so much more of life's abundance, have been making me *keenly* aware of the fact that I exist. All these impressions were perceived, and there can be no perception without existence.

When I write "perceived," perhaps I really mean *felt*, for Sri Yukteswar says, paraphrasing the above: *feeling makes existence conscious*. By extension, the more our feelings are attuned to a spiritual presence in nature and within us—which he calls "the Father"—the more our consciousness expands. This attunement of feelings, too, is called devotion.

Looked at from this grand perspective, love is no longer an instinct for physical survival, it is, indeed, a heavenly gift of nature, for the unfoldment of our innate spirituality.

There is really nothing pious or hypocritical about true devotion. It is not lip service to the church, offered through endless mumbled prayers. Nor is it an emotionally charged sermon shouted from a pulpit. It isn't even the wonderful enthusiasm we may feel at the beginning of our spiritual quest. It is rather the determination, on the battlefield of daily life, to focus resolutely on such qualities as peace, divine love, self-control, and light.

The feminine part within us tends to focus on our present feelings as our ultimate reality. "I feel what I feel, and I cannot feel what I don't feel," is the rationalization behind this attitude. Feeling is, by nature, peremptory. "Convinced against its will, it is of the same opinion still."

On the other hand, once nature has evolved to the level of the human species, it continually urges us to expand our consciousness, and this process has to involve the faculty of feeling. If we accept the idea that the feelings of the heart are multilayered, then we must also accept that one layer of feeling cannot deny the existence of deeper layers. Our reaction to music may very well exemplify this.

I once had a friend who, upon hearing the second movement of Mozart's Piano Concerto no. 21 for the first time, looked as if a new inner world of beauty had opened up for her. An interesting conversation followed.

"How is it possible for anyone to write something so incredibly beautiful?" she asked in amazement after a long silence.

"You have to be beautiful inside to be able to produce something beautiful outside," I answered.

Her subsequent response to my musing did not surprise me, for I knew that she had grown up with few thoughtful, cultured people around her. Her family had been dysfunctional. She felt that life had cheated her, and was generally pessimistic about human nature and about herself. She visibly struggled with her initial reaction to the music that had moved her so deeply and finally said:

"No! This Mozart has simply mastered some very special technical skill!"

I tried to convince her, but to no avail. The vinyl long-play record was put away, and with it, the new wealth of feeling the music had awakened in her heart.

The price for not heeding Nature's call for emotional and spiritual growth is depression, as I soon discovered in my friend.

This conversation took place in the Netherlands, where the prevailing religion, Calvinism, has left little room for feeling. The religious history of my country is all about moral and civic rectitude, hard work, financial stability, and a predestined fate. Jesus is supposed to be the great inspiration of this religion, but I have never understood where he actually fits in this bleak picture. A visit to another land initiated a personal awakening—the innate devotion that I had felt for Jesus as a little child was rekindled by my first journey to Italy, at age seventeen.

After that first journey, it was my heart, much more than my mind, that began to perceive the possibility of a consciousness greater than the limitations of ego, which had previously seemed inextricable. This deeply felt intuition led me towards Eastern philosophy, without estranging me from the sense of Jesus dwelling in my heart. When I first started reading about Swami Sri Yukteswar, in Yogananda's *Autobiography of a Yogi*, the stories about this great Master of wisdom evoked a heartfelt awareness of ancient memories.

The same feeling still arises when this great Master wraps his aura around me through that little booklet that he wrote—to which this book of homage is dedicated. Again, I can by no means claim that I understand every word of *The Holy Science*, yet I do feel that his light of wisdom gradually spiritualizes all the living atoms in my heart, in the stages that he himself identifies.

I become enthused; I steady my enthusiasm through efforts to follow his instructions. I cultivate a desire to turn within. I develop devotion.

Devotion, Sri Yukteswar teaches us, is the heart's desire for connection with the inner realities of the soul. The mental focus required to satisfy this desire gradually frees the heart of what oppresses it. This process particularly draws our attention to the "north" or positive pole of the sixth chakra—the *ajna* chakra, often called the spiritual eye, or the "third eye"—located at the point between the eyebrows.

Before we end this chapter with additional thoughts from Sri Yukteswar, let us imagine that we are standing at the entrance door to an unknown astral land of rare natural beauty and of spiritual possibilities beyond our dreams. The colors, the sounds, and the fragrances permeating the air elevate our consciousness to a level where we can perceive the union between Spirit and the *Prakriti* he has defined. The nourishment of this astral visit is a thousand times more satisfying than the most exquisite meal prepared for us on earth. Sri Yukteswar wants us to open that door. The following inspirational lines paraphrase his instructions in *The Holy Science*:

> By concentrating on the spiritual eye and by remaining centered in the spine, you will become baptized or absorbed in a holy stream of the Divine Sound. This baptism is called Bhakti Yoga. In this

state you will make a definitive change of direction: turning from this gross material creation of Darkness, Maya, you will climb back toward your own Divinity, your Eternal Father, whom you had left.

Part Four

THREE HELPFUL PRACTICES

CHAPTER EIGHTEEN

Introduction to Three Helpful Practices

I N RELATIVELY FEW PAGES, we have come a long way togeth-er. How are you doing at this point? Do you sense the possibility—whether remote or imminent—that, like my little boy many years ago, you might someday look at yourself upon waking up and say, "I have grown"? The chances are good; even a little portion of these teachings of wisdom and introspection can transform some of the heavy lead in our subconscious mind into the shining gold of peace. The additional good news is that the changes, as small and insignificant as they may seem, are permanent. There is no regress in the science of Self-realization: imma-turity can grow towards maturity, but maturity can never lead to immaturity.

Also, let's remember that our goal is the pursuit of happi-ness through wisdom. Happiness, Sri Yukteswar says, comes with the awakening of the heart's natural love, which man-ifests the bliss of our own being. If we never lose sight of that goal, we will always have something to live for—and to strive for.

And all this can occur exactly where you are. There is no need to make dramatic changes in your life, such as withdrawing from the turmoil of the world to become a hermit or a monk. That expression of spirituality largely belongs to the past. You can stay where you are and create a space in your heart where no one else enters, except you. Here, you can return at any moment of the day, if only for a few minutes, and ask yourself: What is wise in this situation? You can regulate your breath, cool your nervous system, and gain some perspective. Whatever your role in society, these teachings remain available to you and can be practiced within the sovereign domain of your own mind.

Do you recall how we, previously, compared the teachings to the navigation system in your car? You only need to declare or type in the destination and then follow the instructions. Extending this metaphor, you will probably need a car with a gear stick. During this journey of self-inquiry, you must use both feet to move forward; and you should know how and when to change gears, by learning to listen to the sound of your "inner engine." Then the task is to remain attentive to the spoken instructions.

If you fail to follow the instructions, owing to either incomplete understanding or distracted attention, there will be no eternal hellfire for you, no need for *mea culpa* or for self-chastisement. Even if you drift away for miles from your final destination, all the system will do is recalculate and instruct you how to move closer again.

To complete the metaphor, in the process of drifting away from your destination instead of moving closer to it, you may find fewer gas stations along the road; you might even reach the point of seeking the next station while proceeding on foot with an empty fuel can! Thus time may be lost through failure to follow the instructions, and perhaps even more time to get back on the right trajectory again. However, a feature of the *spiritual* journey is that, with each inch of progress toward your goal, you will receive more fuel, more energy and more joy, hardly perceptible at the beginning, and then steadily increasing with each step forward.

Now that we have studied the "meannesses" that oppress the heart's natural love, and described the stages of its natural unfoldment, let's look at three further points that Sri Yukteswar makes to overcome the meannesses and to develop moral vigor. They may be compared to the instructions of our navigation system. The first of them regards patience.

CHAPTER NINETEEN

Patience, To Transcend Time

> So many people waste their time
> trying to do things quickly!
>
> — PARAMHANSA YOGANANDA

FROM 1940 TO 1945, the Netherlands was occupied by the Nazis, who imposed their hateful ideology on our population. As a child, I heard many sad stories about deportations, summary executions, bombings, and hunger. What struck me most was my father's exclamation: *There was no hindsight. You never knew when all this misery would end!*

Thus suffering is twofold: One is the physical or mental pain; the other is caused by the uncertainty over duration. You never know when the pain will end. In the heat of the emotion that characterizes suffering, you can't wait *until* it ends, you don't *want* to wait—and yet you *are* waiting, even anxiously so, as the painful situation persists. From this perspective, impatience is aroused by an unfulfilled desire, with the concomitant results of frustration and anger.

Sri Yukteswar has a beautiful Sanskrit word for time. He calls it *Kala*, the idea of change in the Ever-Unchangeable.

So time, then, is change, which is a mighty factor in human love. Among newlywed spouses there is often an unfortunate clash of expectations: He thinks she will never change. She hopes he will change. Of course, the opposite usually happens—She changes, he does not.

Time rules our social life through its usual instruments: alarm clocks, watches, calendars, agendas, timelines, reminders. The only occasions when we don't look at our watches are when we sleep, when we distract ourselves with movies and social media, or when we are in the process of satisfying a desire. Sleep may refresh us; distracting fillers may offer some amusement; the satisfaction of a desire may bring some temporary relief. Yet none of these engagements will expand our awareness, and the heart's deeper feelings remain buried under the layers of so much habit-driven, compulsive restlessness.

Thus, our relationship with time is an important aspect of our pursuit of happiness through wisdom. I remember at the age of sixteen having a job in a notary's office in Amsterdam. I bravely toiled until the end of each workday, but the afternoon hours were particularly hard to endure. A million times I looked at the clock, but the minute hand seemed forever hindered, let alone the hour hand!

In hindsight, I've often thought that I could have been so happy during those hours, had I simply relaxed the feelings in my heart! Instead, I held on to mental tension, and postponed my happiness to a later hour that would never come.

Concentration and relaxation are the only real time-masters, and our capacity to employ them depends on the persistence of our tendency to resort to fillers. Concentration and relaxation are closely interrelated: by consciously relaxing the grip of emotional attachments on our burdened heart, our focus on anything we choose becomes ever new. A strong focus on one thing at a time can take the mind to those depths where the storms of emotions, and the ripples of restlessness plaguing the surface, aren't even perceived anymore.

Time poses a mighty threat to human love. The innocent, lovable infant reaches his teenage years and becomes an alien in the home; romantic memories of courting days become buried under the weight of dirty diapers, mortgages, and tax payments. Women face the emotional challenges of menopause, while men often deal with other forms of midlife crises. If we live long enough, old age, more than anything else, shows all of us the ravaging effects of time. Only unruffled patience, both in enjoyment and in suffering, gives us the power to transcend these degradations.

I once heard a story about the Buddha, in his younger years, visiting a town where lived a beautiful courtesan. She had heard about the beauty of the princely master and sent her servants to him with an invitation to come to her mansion. Buddha's followers, knowing the woman's reputation, were shocked to see that their master was ready to comply. They tried to dissuade him, but he, undeterred, was already on his way.

At her elegant mansion, the courtesan passionately declared her love to her beautiful visitor. He reciprocated her love, but declined her plea to become his lover, saying: not now. After a while he left her to join his group of followers.

Thirty years later, they returned to the same town. The Buddha, remembering his promise to the courtesan, immediately went to her home. The stately mansion was now in ruins and Buddha found the woman, sick with leprosy and hideously disfigured, lying all alone on her bed and waiting for death to come and free her.

When she saw and recognized the man whom she had wanted as her lover, there was a spark of hope in her eyes, but remembering her terrible condition, she said, "Don't come near me. I am sick and it's contagious."

"My beloved, I have come to fulfill my promise. Now I can be your lover." Having said that, the Buddha healed the woman with a tender kiss on her forehead. She then became his disciple and followed him, all over ancient India.

Buddha in this story stands for patience, and patience for the power to choose love under all circumstances. Thus patience becomes the lifeguard of the natural love of the heart.

CHAPTER TWENTY:

Swadhiyaya — Deep Study

> Wisdom is not assimilated with the eyes,
> but with the atoms.
>
> —SWAMI SRI YUKTESWAR

GREAT WRITERS INVARIABLY SHARE what we may call adventures in awareness. A story or a poem, in its formative stage in the author's mind, is always preceded by a period of natural, inner growth. Then, the creative act of writing further stimulates this process. Self-expression and self-knowledge usually go hand in hand.

The subjects don't need to be overtly spiritual. Awareness is an elevating factor in even the most mundane life situations. Whatever we do, can proceed from little or great awareness. Even if the characters of a novel are remarkably ignorant and unaware, their portraits are offered with the awareness of what that ignorance signifies in a greater reality.

The deeper the awareness of the artist, the stronger will be the communicative power of their works. We recognize ourselves in the impressions that we receive. Deeper feelings may be awakened that we were not even aware of, and that have nevertheless been intrinsic parts of our consciousness. Unless we suppress the feelings that arise, such as my unfortunate friend did after her heart's brief awakening to the beauty of Mozart's music, these feelings promote change and growth in our souls. Whether the effect is subtle or great, we will never be the same again.

What, then, is the difference between scripture and other forms of great literature?

Scripture is based, not on the maturation of the human ego, but on man's complete transcendence of ego consciousness. It not only inspires, it also instructs. On the one hand, this gives it a peremptory ring, which the ego doesn't always appreciate. On the other hand, it stimulates our awareness of the spiritual riches that await us beyond ego consciousness.

The "peremptory ring" in the previous paragraph could more aptly be called a vibrant gong, whose sound has reverberated throughout the ages, in many facets of humanity's social, artistic, and spiritual life. Initially, this influence was confined and filtered by religious dogmatism. These confines were subsequently challenged by science, thereby laying waste to many old dogmatic forms. In the process, the essential spiritual contents were set free to spread their wings in search of receptive minds.

That is how Oppenheimer, the inventor of the atomic

bomb, came to seek solace in India's most important scripture, the Bhagavad Gita. From that ancient text, he seems to identify particularly with Arjuna, "prince of devotees," whose reluctance to kill his evil relatives is met with the stern discipline of his master Krishna. In the eleventh chapter this Guru reveals himself to the disciple in his infinite, formless essence. From that state he says:

> I am Kala; I am Time.
> Disguised as Endless Doom I come.
> I seize, I obliterate.
> Even were you not to fight,
> (your) foes (. . .) would perish, Arjuna,
> Slain by My mighty will.

Oppenheimer, however, in quoting these verses, speaks not of time, but of death. The line "Now I am become death, the destroyer of worlds" emphasizes the most dramatic change that time can bring.

There are very few, if any, Western composers whose music is not influenced and inspired to some degree by the power of scripture.

A certain Dutch novelist, an avowed atheist, once exclaimed in amazement: "There is nothing about Bach's life that I could feel any affinity with, and yet his music can bring me into a state of sheer ecstasy!"

Apparently, the authenticity of Bach's spiritual inspiration managed to break through the atheistic shield of this otherwise grumpy novelist.

Jesus's words can be traced in many great works of literature—often as an influence or a nuance, but also in some overt ways. One of the most famous passages in nineteenth-century literature can be found in Dostoyevsky's *Crime and Punishment*. A student who has committed a terrible crime seeks solace and support from a young prostitute. He asks her to read her favorite passage from the Gospels. After some initial resistance she reads to him a Biblical narrative that rings with hope for redemption—not only for herself, but also for the troubled student, whom she loves. At the end of the story, both the reader and the listener are transfixed by its power.

> "That is all about the raising of Lazarus," she whispered severely and abruptly, and turning away she stood motionless, not daring to raise her eyes to him. She still trembled feverishly. The candle-end was flickering out in the battered candlestick, dimly lighting up in the poverty-stricken room the murderer and the harlot who had so strangely been reading together the eternal book. Five minutes or more passed.

Thus, scripture is the great mirror of revealed wisdom, held before its readers, so that they may discover their own highest potential. No matter how far you may have strayed from your destination, scripture is there for you, to bring you solace, guidance and inspiration and, to paraphrase Sri Yukteswar, to spiritualize the atoms of your body.

But how do we study scripture? How does it fit into our busy lives? We touched on that a little at the beginning of this book. The importance of reading cannot be over-stated. Friendly voices reach out to you across the ages, to break your loneliness and to nurture you with wisdom. Sri Yukteswar calls this type of study *Swadhiyaya*—that is read-ing or hearing spiritual truth, pondering it, and forming a definite conception of it.

> Sri Yukteswar directed the study of his own disci-ples by the . . . intensive method of one-pointedness. "Wisdom is not assimilated with the eyes, but with the atoms," he said. "When your conviction of a truth is not merely in your brain but in your being, you may diffidently vouch for its meaning." *

Another key may be found in the experience I shared with you in chapter one of this book. The child that read Jesus'

---

* Yogananda, *Autobiography of a Yogi.*

sermon on the mount did not possess the intellectual capacity to understand those vibrant words, and yet they stirred enthusiasm within him. Isn't that in itself a sign that *some* form of deeper understanding must have been transmitted?

This "method" of studying would reflect what Jesus says to his Heavenly Father:

> At that time Jesus answered and said, I thank thee, O Father, Lord of heaven and earth, because thou hast hid these things from the wise and prudent, and hast revealed them unto babes. (Matt 11:25)

At this point, combining the two methods mentioned above, I would like to invite you to share an experiment with me. I will cite below the majestic opening lines of *The Holy Science,* and you will read them for a week or two, with an open heart and a mind free of intellectual resistance or restlessness. It will not take more than two or three minutes at a time. You can read it first thing in the morning, between one phone call and another, on the bus, in a private spot in your house that is otherwise filled with guests, before or after a meditation or a yoga session, and perhaps most effectively, before you go to sleep. Every now and then, observe what these words activate within your heart. At the end of this experiment, prepare a short description of your inner process, or write a poem about it. Keep the experiment a secret.

Man possesses eternal faith and believes intuitively in the existence of a Substance, of which the objects of sense — sound, touch, sight, taste and smell, the component parts of the visible world — are but properties. As man identifies himself with his material body, composed of the aforesaid properties, he is able to comprehend by these imperfect organs these properties only, and not the Substance to which these properties belong. The Eternal Father, God, the only substance in the universe, is therefore not comprehensible by man of this material world, unless he becomes divine by lifting himself above this creation of Darkness or Maya. See Hebrews 11:1 and John 8:28.

"Now faith is the substance of things hoped for, the evidence of things not seen."

"Then said Jesus unto them: When you have lifted up the Son of man, then shall ye know that I am he."*

* Yukteswar, *The Holy Science.*

CHAPTER TWENTY-ONE

Listening

I can hear the sea
Like no one else can.
Who still remembers his own life.

—From PROFESSION OF SILENCE by A. ROLAND HOLST

I**T WOULD BE INTERESTING** to investigate how much of the music echoing in our subconscious minds has entered there by our own free, conscious choice, and how much was absorbed by random exposure. Music is present in almost every sphere of our activities: in supermarkets, in restaurants, in our cars, for commercial spots, on airplanes, during workouts. All of it is stored in that huge warehouse we call the subconscious mind, from which it may rise to the surface involuntarily, usually by spontaneous association.

Lately, melodies have surfaced in my mind from songs that I used to listen to when I was a teenager. It is often a neutral experience, engendering little or no growth. In fact, it may take considerable mental energy to get rid of these "earworms." Sometimes I also do a little self-analysis, so as to understand what part of my consciousness this music represents, why it surfaces at a given moment, and what the particular musical attachment tells me about myself. Then I gain a little self-knowledge in the process.

In any case, the subconscious mind is certainly not the most original part of our consciousness. Whether it mechanically repeats melodies from the past, or keeps us mentally engaged in old memories, resentments, nostalgia, or regret, the subconscious mind tends to bind us to our habitual self, the ego.

These things are particularly felt when we sit down to meditate. We are instructed to listen for something else, something specific, but our attempts are thwarted by a million worries, thoughts, desires—even melodies. If you are just starting to integrate the practice of meditation in your life, and this happens to you (which it will), it is important to realize that this is a good thing. It is only when we open the door to our cellar after many years, that we realize what condition it is in. The cellar in itself doesn't hold any particular interest for us in this metaphor for meditation, because it is the roof where we want to go: there we can gain a panoramic view of the endless space surrounding us, and experience the joy of higher states of consciousness. But in the process, other parts of the house will draw our attention, including the important but often neglected cellar.

It takes patience to accept that, in our attempts to climb higher, there will be distractions. We need to bear with them, sometimes by ignoring them, sometimes with resistant force. But as we said in a previous chapter: patience and calm acceptance will give us the strength to overcome all limitations to our consciousness.

The central feature of this book has been the practice of introspection—the calm yet eager search for truth and authenticity. The stories that I have shared with you are the fruit of this mental practice, which invariably has a meditative character.

Meditation itself plays an important role in the awakening of the heart's natural love. For Sri Yukteswar it primarily means listening for and merging into a uniquely perceived inner sound. This sonority is altogether different from the memories of beautiful music and earworms that linger unbidden in our minds. We will explore this transcendent sound more deeply at the end of this chapter, as we extend our previous experimentation with *Swadhiyaya*, deep study.

For now, let's turn our attention to the role of listening in matters concerning love. This facet has not always been easy for me, for my creative and ambitious mind tends to follow its own uncommon thought-roads. Nevertheless, life has taught me an important universal lesson regarding listening as an active component of love.

I was once sharing a conversation with the director of my spiritual community. At some point she looked at me keenly and then said, "If you don't learn to listen to others, you lose a lot."

She has always been an important source of inspiration for me. I admire her capacity to understand and accept people where they are in their development. I find her remarkably intuitive; her feedback tends to broaden my horizons. Her leadership has forged a most beautiful community. So somehow when she spoke those words, the power behind them opened not only my ears, but also my heart. I have always remembered them.

The willingness to listen to others entails the capacity to let go of our own mental and emotional agenda, so that we can be fully in the here and now with the people in front of us. Our best gift for those whom we love—children, partners, friends, colleagues—is our willingness to listen. The absence of this quality will probably lead to crisis. If the incoming interpersonal signals are repeatedly lost in the fog of our lack of attention, frustration builds up. Joint progress becomes increasingly difficult, and some form of emotional separation ensues. Once the energy goes in that direction, the gap can only widen.

Sri Yukteswar says that the same has happened in our relationship with God. We have lost the capacity to listen. Our own agenda leads us away from Him. If we want to make

Him our destination once more, we need to pay heed to the instructions of our inner navigation system. We need to find moments of silence on the battlefield of our daily lives.

With these cautionary notes in mind, let us finish this chapter then, with another passage from *The Holy Science*. Let us read it for a few weeks with complete focus and child-like openness.

> By . . . concentration of the self on the sensori-um, man becomes baptized or absorbed in the holy stream of the Divine Sound . . . in this state man repents: that is, turning from this gross material creation of darkness . . . he climbs back toward his Divinity, the Eternal Father, whence he had fallen, and passing through the sensorium, the door, enters into an internal sphere . . . . This entrance into the internal world is the second birth of man. In this state man becomes Devata, a divine being.

CONCLUSION

L AST NIGHT I TOOK my sons and a friend of mine to a
Chinese restaurant for dinner. Our conversation included intense dynamics over an uncomfortable issue that rose
to the surface.

My friend and I share a similar life experience: each of us
has endured a divorce from the mother of our children. We
both experienced the pain of loss, separation, and seeming
injustice. After my friend's initial rocky period of adjust-
ment to "life after divorce," one family matter took a turn
for the worse. Over a year has passed since he last saw his
twenty-year-old daughter and his seventeen-year-old son. He
feels deeply hurt by their complete lack of outreach; in return, he now proudly refuses to reach out to them.

The topic hit close to home for my sons and stirred my
concerns. But for my friend the wound was fresh and he
seemed compelled and determined to share his vicissitudes
with us, so we had no choice but to relate to him and his
grievances.

At a certain point, my younger son (recently turned
twenty-three) said, "They are not communicating with you
now, but maybe later they will. They will change, because

now they are still young. And if you keep sending them messages every now and then, later it will be easier for them to reach out to you."

And my older son (twenty-five) offered: "*You* should make them feel that you are happy and strong. My relationship with him (indicating me, his father) was very difficult for me, and I did not want to go to stay with him. We, too, were brainwashed by our mother and her family for a period of time. But that changed when I began to see that my father is doing well with the life he has chosen—that he feels realized."

Over the past several months my work on this book, in the company of Sri Yukteswar, has helped to uplift my consciousness. The effect this has had on me showed when, at a certain point in the dinner conversation, I heard myself say: "I understand that you feel hurt, but you should get over your pride and send them regular messages. Whether they reply or not, make them feel that you are there, and that they are important to you. And that you are well and calm and strong, having overcome most of the pain and trouble related to your divorce. That way you will plant seeds of love in their hearts, and when the time is ready, those seeds will inevitably sprout."

Possibly the least ego-gratifying manifestation of love is the one between parents and their children. Teenagers are especially unlikely to give any bonuses to their parents. Yet their seeming indifference betrays their vulnerability and their unspoken need for understanding and clarity. Sometimes all we can do is give them ample space with our love and, from that distance, help them feel that we are there for them.

This strategy is not nearly as cold and detached as it may sound. Distance generally allows for a more expansive view and facilitates listening for issues that lurk beneath the surface. Thus the efforts we make to detach ourselves emotionally from our dear ones may actually be a sign of love. We can be of much more help to them if we don't allow our own desires and attachments to interfere in our relationships with them.

This very recent episode from my life carries us closer to the expanded perspective that we have sought to gain. All the stories that you have read in this book, from beginning to end, are about the natural love of the heart and how to awaken it. They are offered with my utmost sincerity. In sharing them, I have felt light and happy and inspired by a sense of deep connection with eternal truths. I hope they have provided some guidance and entertainment for your journey through this life.

I also trust that Swami Sri Yukteswar, the central inspiration of this work, has touched your soul and gained entrance into your home, as a friend and teacher—capable of prompting winning strategies for you on the battlefield of life. Although he never physically ventured outside India, his teachings will continue to reach countless truth seekers all over the world. Bear in mind: His name signifies union (yuk) with Iswara (ஈஸ்வரன்), which is God as divine Light.

May that Light shine upon you, in your ongoing pursuit of happiness through wisdom.

Swami Sri Yukteswar's Seaside Hermitage in Puri, India.

FURTHER EXPLORATIONS

CRYSTAL CLARITY PUBLISHERS

If you enjoyed this title, Crystal Clarity Publishers invites you to deepen your spiritual life through many additional resources based on the teachings of Paramhansa Yogananda. We offer books, e-books, audiobooks, yoga and meditation videos, and a wide variety of inspirational and relaxation music composed by Swami Kriyananda.

See a listing of books below, visit our secure website for a complete online catalog, or place an order for our products.

crystalclarity.com | clarity@crystalclarity.com

800.424.1055 | 1123 Goodrich Blvd. | Commerce, CA 90022

ANANDA WORLDWIDE

Crystal Clarity Publishers is the publishing house of Ananda, a worldwide spiritual movement founded by Swami Kriyananda, a direct disciple of Paramhansa Yogananda. Ananda offers resources and support for your spiritual journey through meditation instruction, webinars, online virtual community, email, and chat.

Ananda has more than 150 centers and meditation groups in over 45 countries, offering group guided meditations, classes and teacher training in meditation and yoga, and many other resources.

In addition, Ananda has developed eight residential communities in the US, Europe, and India. Spiritual communities are places where people live together in a spirit of cooperation and friendship, dedicated to a common goal. Spirituality is practiced in all areas of daily life: at school, at work, or in the home. Many Ananda communities offer internships during which one can stay and experience spiritual community firsthand.

For more information about Ananda communities or meditation groups near you, please visit ananda.org or call 530.478.7560.

THE EXPANDING LIGHT RETREAT

The Expanding Light is the largest retreat center in the world to share exclusively the teachings of Paramhansa Yogananda. Situated in the Ananda Village community near Nevada City, California, the center offers the opportunity to experience spiritual life in a contemporary ashram setting. The varied, year-round schedule of classes and programs on yoga, meditation, and spiritual practice includes Karma Yoga, personal retreat, spiritual travel, and online learning. Large groups are welcome.

The Ananda School of Yoga & Meditation offers certified yoga, yoga therapist, spiritual counselor, and meditation teacher trainings.

The teaching staff has years of experience practicing Kriya Yoga meditation and all aspects of Paramhansa Yogananda's teachings. You may come for a relaxed personal renewal, participating in ongoing activities as much or as little as you wish. The serene mountain setting, supportive staff, and delicious vegetarian meals provide an ideal environment for a truly meaningful stay, be it a brief respite or an extended spiritual vacation.

For more information, please visit expandinglight.org or call 800.346.5350.

ANANDA MEDITATION RETREAT

Set amidst seventy-two acres of beautiful meditation gardens and wild forest in Northern California's Sierra foothills, the Ananda Meditation Retreat is an ideal setting for a rejuvenating, inner experience.

The Meditation Retreat has been a place of deep meditation and sincere devotion for over fifty years. Long before that, the Native American Maidu tribe held this to be sacred land. The beauty and presence of the Divine are tangibly felt by all who visit here.

Studies show that being in nature and using techniques such as forest bathing can significantly reduce stress and blood pressure while strengthening your immune system, concentration, and level of happiness. The Meditation Retreat is the perfect place for quiet immersion in nature.

Plan a personal retreat, enjoy one of the guided retreats, or choose from a variety of programs led by the caring and joyful staff.

For more information or to place your reservation, please visit meditationretreat.org, email meditationretreat@ananda.org, or call 530.478.7557.

THE ORIGINAL 1946 UNEDITED EDITION OF
YOGANANDA'S SPIRITUAL MASTERPIECE

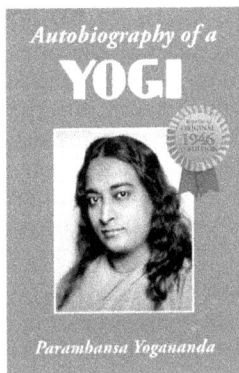

AUTOBIOGRAPHY OF A YOGI
Paramhansa Yogananda

Autobiography of a Yogi is one of the world's most acclaimed spiritual classics, with millions of copies sold. Named one of the Best 100 Spiritual Books of the twentieth century, this book helped launch and continues to inspire a spiritual awakening throughout the Western world.

Yogananda was the first yoga master of India whose mission brought him to settle and teach in the West. His firsthand account of his life experiences in India includes childhood revelations, stories of his visits to saints and masters, and long-secret teachings of yoga and Self-realization that he first made available to the Western reader.

This reprint of the original 1946 edition is free from textual changes made after Yogananda's passing in 1952. This updated edition includes bonus materials: the last chapter that Yogananda wrote in 1951, also without posthumous changes, the eulogy Yogananda wrote for Gandhi, and a new foreword and afterword by Swami Kriyananda, one of Yogananda's close, direct disciples.

Also available in Spanish and Hindi from Crystal Clarity Publishers.

SCIENTIFIC HEALING AFFIRMATIONS
Paramhansa Yogananda

Yogananda's 1924 classic, reprinted here, is a pioneering work in the fields of self-healing and self-transformation. He explains that words are crystallized thoughts and have life-changing power when spoken with conviction, concentration, willpower, and feeling. Yogananda offers far more than mere suggestions for achieving positive attitudes. He shows how to impregnate words with spiritual force to shift habitual thought patterns of the mind and create a new personal reality.

Added to this text are over fifty of Yogananda's well-loved "Short Affirmations," taken from issues of *East-West* and *Inner Culture* magazines from 1932 to 1942. This little book will be a treasured companion on the road to realizing your highest, divine potential.

METAPHYSICAL MEDITATIONS
Paramhansa Yogananda

Metaphysical Meditations is a classic collection of meditation techniques, visualizations, affirmations, and prayers from the great yoga master, Paramhansa Yogananda. The meditations given are of three types: those spoken to the individual consciousness, prayers or demands addressed to God, and affirmations that bring us closer to the Divine.

Select a passage that meets your specific need and speak each word slowly and purposefully until you become absorbed in its inner meaning. At the bedside, by the meditation seat, or while traveling—one can choose no better companion than *Metaphysical Meditations*.

CONVERSATIONS WITH YOGANANDA

Stories, Sayings, and Wisdom of Paramhansa Yogananda
Recorded with reflections, by his disciple, Swami Kriyananda

For those who enjoyed Paramhansa Yogananda's autobiography and long for more, this collection of conversations offers rare intimate glimpses of life with the Master as never before shared.

This is an unparalleled account of Yogananda and his teachings written by one of his foremost disciples. Swami Kriyananda was often present when Yogananda spoke privately with other close disciples, received visitors and answered their questions, and dictated and discussed his writings. He recorded the Master's words, preserving a treasure trove of wisdom that would otherwise have been lost.

These Conversations include not only Yogananda's words as he spoke them, but the added insight of a disciple who spent over fifty years attuning his consciousness to that of his guru.

The collection features nearly five hundred stories, sayings, and insights from the twentieth century's most famous master of yoga, as well as twenty-five photos — nearly all previously unreleased.

WHISPERS FROM ETERNITY

A Book of Answered Prayers
Paramhansa Yogananda
Edited by his disciple, Swami Kriyananda

Many poetic works can inspire, but few have the power to change lives. These poems and prayers have been "spiritualized" by Paramhansa Yogananda: Each has drawn a response from the Divine. Yogananda was not only a master poet, whose imagery here is as vivid and alive as when first published in 1949: He was a spiritual master, an avatar.

He encouraged his disciples to read from *Whispers from Eternity* every day, explaining that through these verses he could guide them after his passing. But this book is not for his disciples alone. It is for spiritual aspirants of any tradition who wish to drink from this fountain of pure inspiration and wisdom.

YOUR SUN SIGN AS A SPIRITUAL GUIDE
Swami Kriyananda

In this book, Swami Kriyananda shows how, with awareness, attention, and will, one can cultivate the higher potential of a person's sign rather than being limited by its karmic energy, leading to greater fulfillment and success. We can learn to work with these energies and develop their more refined, higher octaves, which will then magnetize new possibilities into our lives.

Kriyananda's approach is to encourage and inspire one's Self to awaken, and to express itself through the sun sign. Within each of us is vast potential to be awakened. Your Sun Sign as a Spiritual Guide is an inspiring book that will open doors and encourage one in this direction.

Yogic understanding is rich and often runs counter to prevailing thought. So too with astrology, the reader will find vistas of understanding opening as Kriyananda takes the words and guidance of this yogic view of astrology to heart. This book reassures the reader that sun-sign weaknesses can be spiritual strengths if pursued rightly. It also warns one not to rest on the laurels of sun-sign strengths, but to go much deeper. Concentrated, deep wisdom is available to the seeker in this brief, easy-to-digest book that helps the reader to understand himself and others from a higher perspective.

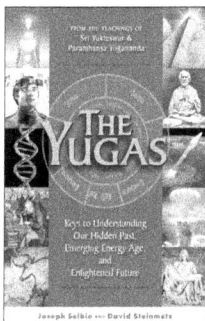

THE YUGAS

Keys to Understanding Our Hidden Past, Emerging
Energy Age, and Enligtened Future
Joseph Selbie and David Steinmetz

With far-reaching changes happening on virtually
a daily basis, many are wondering if we are due for
a world-changing global shift, and what the future
holds for mankind. Paramhansa Yogananda (author of the classic Autobiography of a Yogi) and his
teacher, Sri Yukteswar, offered key insights into this
subject nearly a century ago.

They presented a fascinating explanation of the rising and falling eras
that our planet cycles through every 24,000 years. According to their
teachings, we have recently passed through the low ebb in that cycle and
are moving forward to a higher age—an Energy Age that will revolution-
ize the world. They declared that we would live in a time of great social
and spiritual change, and that much of what we believed to be fixed and
true—our entire way of looking at the world—would ultimately be trans-
formed and uplifted.

In The Yugas, Joseph Selbie and David Steinmetz present substantial and
intriguing evidence from the findings of historians and scientists that
demonstrate the truth of Yukteswar and Yogananda's revelations.

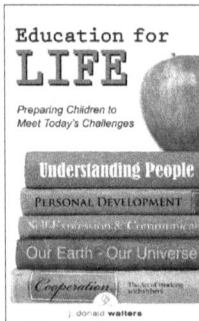

EDUCATION FOR LIFE
Preparing Children to Meet Today's Challenges
J. Donald Walters (Swami Kriyananda)

Education for Life offers a constructive and brilliant alternative to what has been called the disaster of modern education. The need for a change is universally recognized. The statistics of illiteracy, drug abuse, and violence speak for themselves. In this book, Kriyananda traces the problems to an emphasis on technological competence at the expense of spiritual values, which alone can give higher meaning to life. *Education for Life* offers parents, educators, and concerned citizens everywhere techniques that are both compassionate and practical.

Based on the pioneering work in India of Paramhansa Yogananda in the early twentieth century, this book offers a workable combination of idealism and practicality, telling educators what to teach, when to teach it, how to teach it, and why. The *Education for Life* system has been tested and proven for over five decades at Living Wisdom Schools both in the United States and in Europe.

Parents and educators have acclaimed these schools as places where children are encouraged to grow toward full maturity as human beings: where they learn not only facts, but what it takes to become the kind of empowered people who live successful, happy, fulfilled lives, and who serve as blessings on the communities in which they live.

www.ingramcontent.com/pod-product-compliance
Lightning Source LLC
Chambersburg PA
CBHW072143090426
42739CB00013B/3268